Children of the Revolution

CHILDREN OF THE REVOLUTION

PHIL COHEN

Lawrence & Wishart, London

Lawrence & Wishart
99a Wallis Road, London E9 5LN

First published 1997
by Lawrence & Wishart

ISBN 0 85315 841 X

Brtitish Library Cataloguing
in Publication data
A catalogue record for this book
is available from the British Library

Typesetting Art Services, Norwich
Printed and bound in Great Britain
by Redwood Books, Trowbridge.

CONTENTS

FOREWORD

GILLIAN SLOVO

There was a moment during my mother's funeral in Mozambique when I found myself taking in an involuntary breath. I was standing in the family line up, listening to a succession of speeches about the heroic martyr rather than the mother I had known, when one of the speakers got specific: he chose as his highest compliment and the peak of his oratory, the fact that Ruth had been an exemplary Communist. What surprised me was not that he thought of her that way but rather my own reaction: I was shocked that he had used the C word in public.

Looking back, I can still marvel at my response. After all, neither of my parents had ever made a secret of their party membership - how could they when they were named, banned and denigrated as reds in every South African newspaper? My mother was hardly exemplary - nothing stopped her from voicing her criticisms of the Soviet Union - but she was still a defiant Communist. And yet at her funeral, when one of her comrades named her thus, it felt to me as if something forbidden and dangerous had been inadvertently let loose.

I realised then how far one of the tentacles of our childhood's many unspoken rules had been stretched. We children of reds belonged to a unique world, a world of sacrifice and secrecy and conspiracy. When I was growing up in South Africa my parents had a desk with a specially constructed, hidden compartment in which they kept banned literature: meanwhile, thousands of miles away in America, a friend's parents hid their party newspaper in the freezer. We all belonged to a conspiracy and yet, at the same time, we were excluded from it. We observed the workings of our parents clandestine world, and we learned to hide what was discussed in the home from people whom we instinctively knew would despise us for it. We were special, we were hated: we were proud of what our parents did and we hid it from the outside world as if we were ashamed. That was our childhood universe which our non commie friends could never have understood.

My parents and their comrades appeared to be so sure of themselves, that they were right in what they did and that they would win. They had standards and they stuck to them - not standards of personal behaviour which could be restricted to an individual, but a morality that embraced a nation.

For a child it was a hard act to follow. How could we not applaud their selflessness? But at the same time how could it not dawn on us that it was this very generosity to others that deprived us of our parents? Their choices gave us a sense of belonging to a group of conspirators who were so close it was like belonging to an extended family, but the same choices meant we in Johannesburg were also cut out of ordinary life. We grew up as the children of rebels; when it was our time to explore the outside world it had irrevocably changed. We had our parents' heroism and their sacrifices as our standard bearers and yet the choices they made were no longer open to us.

These days in Britain it is usually at funerals when it dawns on me that, although I thought I was in the company of strangers, they all seem somehow familiar. It doesn't take me long to work out why: the dead mother of a friend might not have held a party card for at least twenty years. But the people who come to mourn her are nevertheless made utterly distinctive by their long past affiliations. They are English, my parents were South African, and yet they have a way of looking at the world, and a certainty about them, that is unmistakable. I sit and listen to what they say and I am infuriated by their complacency and the self-satisfied certainty by which they feel they can judge the rest of the world, and yet I also feel that I am amongst family, that this universe with its fierce sense of belonging is mine, not because of any choice I made, but because my parents' actions gave me life long membership.

When my father, whose CV had included being both general secretary and chairman of the South African Communist Party, died, the flags that were waved were red, the crepe wreath which was given pride of place had a hammer and sickle at its centre, and the all-African choir sung the Internationale in Xhosa. It felt like an echo from another time, but as I sat watching, my scepticism wrestled with a fondness and a sadness for this world that is now largely gone.

INTRODUCTION

From the day in August 1949 that my parents named me after Phil Piratin, who was then a Communist MP, I was probably fated to produce a book like this. Call it determinism or dialectical materialism or whatever, but when you start off in life with that sort of inheritance it is natural that you puzzle over it and try to make sense of it. Then you realise that there are all sorts of reasons for not opening up the Pandora's box of childhood memories and emotions. I tossed and turned them about for some time, almost as if I was looking for a way out. But once an idea takes hold it is powerful and difficult to shake off.

At one and the same time the subject is complicated and painful and part of the past, yet also endlessly fascinating because it holds the key to how we are now, and will be in the future.

It must have taken two years of self-analysis and discussion with friends and family before I decided to press ahead with the project. Frank Chalmers, a fellow freelance journalist, enthused me with the idea in his inimitable way during several cappuccino sessions; Michael Rosen was marvellously encouraging and helpful, and, fortunately, publishers Lawrence and Wishart displayed the sort of enthusiasm that is infectious and makes you believe you are not just a lone voice. For that I must thank Sally Davison and her total belief in this book.

I realised quite soon that what I was interested in was neither a full-scale survey of CP children nor an academic study. My interview subjects are meant to be a cross-section who give a flavour of what a CP upbringing was like, in as much as one can use that generic description. Considering the variety of backgrounds and areas of the country represented, I was struck by the way certain themes kept recurring, and I hope that, taken as a whole, the interviews enable the reader to build up a mental picture of our generation's peculiar experience.

In the end, despite misgivings that I was treading on dangerous ground, this proved to be a rewarding and satisfying book to put together. It enabled me to meet a group of interesting people that I would otherwise not have met. Their honesty and humour were refreshing and I thank all of them for their candour in describing their relationships with parents and families.

Some people were almost eager to talk about their early lives, as if they had come to a stage where they were able to reflect on what had happened to them; others needed a little more encouragement. A special thanks to Martin Jones who travelled from Germany for his interview, and to Brian Pollitt for giving up an entire day and providing some Glasgwegian hospitality for my benefit.

The interviews are in the first person, set down much as the words were spoken, but with some re-organising and editing, because I felt people should be able to tell their own stories in their own individual way. If the interviewees take centre stage there is another group in the background which must be remembered; the brothers and sisters who all shared the CP experience. In a way this book is for them also.

I also particularly want to thank Barbara Firth who gave me valuable ideas about the structure of the book when I was having one of my several periods of self-doubt, and who later spent some time reading parts of the text and made suggestions which can only have improved it. My sister Norma was a constant source of ideas and inspiration, and has a right to feel the book echoes her experience as much as, if not more than, my own; I want to include my brother Maurice in that too. Thanks also to Bernadette for her encouragement and toleration of my many hours spent interviewing, transcribing and writing, and thank you to my children Stephen and Alice for, well, being Stephen and Alice!

Lastly, my thanks go to my father Eric 'without whom all this would not have been possible,' as they say. He has not once questioned this project or expressed concern about my references to him in it. This could be seen as a deviously clever tactic so as to secure a more favourable comment from me - I prefer to regard it as a sign of his open-mindedness and his encouragement to me, which I value.

I have often taken my stand and pitched my tent against some of the political views he has held and the severe cost of his beliefs to his family, but I have never doubted the sincerity with which he has held those beliefs.

At ten years old I was marching through the centre of Liverpool in the freezing cold, thinking only of what the score at Anfield was and not at all of the effect all these Communists were having on the oppressed proletariat. Finally, as always, we got to the Pier Head, where the marchers lined up facing the speakers for the rally, using the megaphone from a car with a loudspeaker.

A gust of wind chilled me to the bone and made me pull the collar of my school raincoat tighter around my neck. Behind the speakers, tankers and ferries drifted under a grey sky. Everything in Liverpool is grey, I thought, grey shops, grey houses, grey people.

I was writing that in my twenties, looking back on a world that had already gone, a world of childhood in which parents were still the key points of reference, with the CP as an essential backcloth to my life. It was the 1950s then, when some political and ideological certainties remained intact, together with the hope that the old order might still be swept away. But already, unbeknown to me, the Cold War had cast its pall over the communist movement and many individual CP-ers who had made their clear political choices in the halycon days of the 1930s were beginning to have doubts. Even then I was reflecting a certain cynicism about the ritual aspects of CP culture: the marches, the speeches and the time spent away from more hedonistic pursuits.

For our parents these were the essential elements of political life, born out of a hundred campaigns, against fascism and non-intervention in the Spanish Civil War, for deep bomb-proof shelters and the Second Front during the war, for women's rights and better housing after the war. But for the next generation, we children who reached our teens in the 1960s and 1970s, the world was a very different place and the opportunities for education and career advancement much greater.

Of course there were still campaigns - important ones like CND, anti-Vietnam War, the miners' strikes - but the Soviet Union, which had been the beacon of the communist world, became merely a flickering ember. Martin Kettle has written in his *Guardian* column about the difficult inheritance of those growing up since the war, particularly people whose parents had been active in the communist and anti-fascist movements leading up to the war:

> *My generation is in a curious position in relation to the war. We are close to it but we are not part of it ... As a result we grew up as the bearers of an intense memory of things which we ourselves had not experienced. And because we had not experienced them, because we knew from the start that there was always a happy ending, we could not truthfully share the anxieties and make the choices which real individuals have to make in real situations. All we got was the myth. It stopped us from being ourselves. It was an inhibition.*

This is a subtle point. Kettle is not saying that communist parents told us how to think or what to say, although their influence was there around us in the things we talked about, in the very thoughts we had and the choices we made. Values are partly a question of upbringing, affected by what you know will please your parents and the experiences that shape you as a person, which are inevitably bound up with your parents. But the benevolent paternalism of the CP could be stifling to those growing up within it. Teenage rebellion was not easy when you were told that saving the world from imperialism was the key thing in life. Somehow the craving for independence which comes to everyone over 16 could always be absorbed and deflected.

Although we took the idealism and internationalism from our parents, we did not share other prejudices, such as their aversion for all things American. John Kennedy was an inspiration for us, as were the sex, drugs and rock and roll of the time. And we were conscious of a curious attitude to notions of patriotism and nationalism that CP members somehow never resolved. A tendency to despise aspects of British life became intermingled with anger over the appeasement of facism in the 1930s. The KGB moles Philby, Burgess, Maclean, Blunt and others who penetrated the secret service and the establishment, were evidence of a more widespread feeling among the people of my parent's generation, that Britain was rotten while the future lay elsewhere, in the east. In culture and in sport, British communists lauded everything Soviet and East European. This low opinion of one's own country carried over into the post-war years and added to the contradictions within a party taking a specifically British road to socialism, but historically tied to the international communist movement.

There was also a class factor in CP membership. Attitudes towards the Soviet Union, the 'upper classes' and the workplace were inevitably influenced by class origin. Some working-class members seemed to resent the increasing professionalisation of the party, as younger people came through the universities and higher education system in place after the war. Many of my generation were not prepared to explain away or to rationalise the CP's approach to politics, although many wrestled with it before either challenging from within or breaking away. The CP tried to adjust to changes in society, but was too rooted in the drama of the past to relate to the more complex world that was coming.

Another undoubted influence on the party was its Jewish membership, most notably in the East End of London and other areas of Jewish settlement in Britain. To some degree it extended across class divides and represented a significant radical group that not only played a major part in anti-facist work but contributed heavily to the intellectual life of the party. As Jews, the tendency was to attempt to assimilate with British culture and escape the latent anti-semitism which lay hidden below the surface of British life. Arguably this could produce a political outlook driven in two separate directions: the desire to be accepted by the host society and to find a niche within it on the one hand, while holding on to a radical tradition which challenges convention and inequality and wishes to change society. Many

Jewish CP members were socially conservative and deliberately set out to be pillars of the local community, perhaps believing that they could communicate their political message more convincingly. This paradox was not confined to Jews: many communists entrenched themselves in local areas and were popular to the extent that they took up local issues, such as the closure of a library.

One of the reasons for writing this book is that, with the demise of communist parties in Europe (even if they may have been reincarnated as social democratic parties in some countries), our generation will be the last to have this unique kind of upbringing. Growing up in the late twentieth and early twenty-first centuries, our children will inherit a very different world. Not for them the 'absent father' constantly away at conferences and meetings; nor will they be brought up to believe that there is a single world-view that explains everything, surrounded by an obsessive interest - encompassing everything from its films and books to its tractor design - in a foreign country like the Soviet Union. With its inbred idealism, its quasi-religious faith in Russia, and its notion of sacrifice for the good of others, the CP provided a role model which is unlikely to be repeated.

I also feel my generation is inextricably linked to a social history of post-war Britain, a time in which the idealism of the pre-war and war period gradually gave way to a questioning of political faith and a feeling that left politics were under attack from the right. Accompanying that is an insight into families where politics meant personal sacrifice, and in some cases the 'party' and the cause ranked as a higher priority than personal relationships. In this way I hope the book may in a modest sense be of interest to historians and sociologists.

I attempted to test my theses in a series of interviews with people whose parents were in the CP and who were mostly born during or after the war. I found many of the features of my own CP childhood were mirrored in their experiences, although there were differences in individual relationships with parents. Our thinking was influenced by the degree to which our parents became politically disillusioned, and whether we ourselves had joined the Young Communist League (YCL) and the CP, either as a temporary move or because of a specific commitment to change the CP and make it more internally democratic.

For most of the interviewees there had, at some point, been a re-appraisal and a rethinking of the CP inheritance, leading either to a complete rejection of the CP in favour of Trotskyism or Maoism, or a conscious decision to tackle the centrist bureaucracy of the CP. This latter path came from a realisation that certain liberal democratic values were not exclusively 'capitalist' after all: they were the enduring values of human freedom, the right to individual expression and to individual conscience, which should belong to all human beings. If these principles could have been combined with socialist planning, a powerfully appealing synthesis could have been produced, a vision arguably closer to the original ideals of the British socialist movement, which was otherwise perverted by the constant need to follow edicts from Moscow. This reforming mission - described by Bloomfield, Devine and Power in their interviews - was attempted but remained largely unsuccessful, because that trend never captured the party as a whole. Later there was a damaging split from which the CP never recovered.

From a personal standpoint we 'children of the revolution' felt different from our peers in the way we took issue with our teachers, defiantly wore CND badges and defended Russia against verbal abuse. Many of us were taken or sent on holidays in Eastern Europe, which must have appeared rather exotic to our friends playing on the beaches of Blackpool or Bournemouth. We were part of a kind of extended family (Jackie Kay calls it a 'secret society') with a web of social networks that took in party 'socials' and regular *Daily Worker* bazaars. Much of it seemed fun and appealing to the young mind, and at that stage the political aspect took a decided second place to the concerts, banner waving and annual coach trips with a packed lunch.

We were always conscious of the international aspect of the commitment. Communism represented more than a few thousand party members in Britain: the movement embraced sugar cane workers in Cuba, black people without the vote in the USA, peasants fighting colonialism in Vietnam. Unlike our parents' generation, who found in the CP a gateway to movements throughout the world, we were reared on internationalism: it was part of the air we breathed. This upbringing will no longer be an option for future generations.

The CP culture can also be seen in a semi-religious context, with the notion of faith in a greater good, sacrifice for others and pilgrimages to the promised land. Willie Thompson talks about how the lives of willing CP members after the war were totally consumed by meetings and political duties such as door-to-door canvassing, street newspaper sales, poster parades and demonstrations. 'It added up to a regimen that was possible only to sustain by a quasi-religious faith, which like other faiths achieved some of its purposes by the inculcation of personal guilt - for no matter how much you did you always felt guilty for not doing still more; nobody was able to be quite the perfect militant,' he says. This may seem contentious, even provocative, to those who were totally committed to changing society, and it is certainly not my intention to doubt their sincerity. But the analogy with religion, particularly Catholicism, that cropped up in the interviews may help in the struggle to understand one issue that kept recurring in my mind - why did sincere and intelligent people suspend their critical faculties for so long, both in supporting foreign leaders and regimes that were so evidently not worthy of support, and believing that British people would eventually 'see the light' and vote for them? Was it, as Jackie Kay says, that 'love is blind'? It is interesting to note that as soon as Hywel Francis's father joined the CP he stopped going to chapel, but is one a substitute for the other?

Before embarking on this project I hesitated for some time, and the reasons may be relevant. One person who preferred not to take part wrote to me that 'my mother is now 89 years old and she would not approve.' Mothers and fathers are still alive and may take exception to the questioning of political positions or ideas that they held at the time. But is that a reason for rejecting the validity of our experience, which is very different? In the end I thought not.

I also felt the burden of expectation that, in tackling the subject, I could not leave out an examination of the basic roots of the CP in historical terms, which led to its post-war development and the context in which sons and daughters grew up. But there have been recent accounts of CP history in Willie

Thompson's *The Good Old Cause* and Francis Beckett's *Enemy Within*, and the internicine conflicts with Stalin and the Comintern have already been well documented by others more qualified to do so than myself.[1]

The person whose letter is quoted above summed up the theme of this book when he wrote that 'you mention (rightly) the extent to which our childhoods were made up of a mixture of idealism and pretence, and in a book like this I fear that the pretence might emerge again as a fairly dominant theme!' It is that strange combination that fascinates me and I only hope it will interest others, whether they had a 'political' upbringing or not.

NOTE

1. *The Good Old Cause: British Communism 1920-1991*, Pluto Press 1992, page 87. See also Francis Beckett, *Enemy Within: the rise and fall of the British Communist Party*, published by John Murray, 1995.

RED ROOTS
from Lenin to Lennon
PHIL COHEN

MY PARENTS

Eve Cohen, my mother, was born in Liverpool near the docks in 1919. Her father was a salesman and impresario with a passion for music who sang at a local synagogue. Her family was very poor and there was little money to spare for decent clothes, books or entertainment. At one point they were evicted from their corporation house by bailiffs because they could not afford the rent. Her father left the family when Eve was 12, so she had to help her mother bring up her two brothers and a sister.

Leaving school at the age of 17, my mother worked as an office clerk until 1941 when she went to work in an aircraft factory as part of the war effort, becoming a shop steward for the AEU. In 1944, she transferred to another factory which made ships' wirelesses and was again made shop steward.

Eric Cohen, my father, was born in 1912 in Liverpool, where his father owned some shops. His parents had emigrated to Britain to escape the persecution of Jews in Russia and had been influenced by the ideas of the *Bund*, a left-wing Zionist movement. One branch of the family introduced him to Marxism and the CP, and my father became heavily involved in politics as secretary of Liverpool YCL and secretary of the Friends of the Soviet Union. He joined the CP in the 1930s when fascism threatened the Spanish Republic, and says he would have gone to Spain to fight if the party had asked him to.

My father was articled to a firm of chartered accountants in Liverpool and later worked for the Liverpool Typographical Society, which was a forerunner of first ASTMS, and then the MSF union; he has therefore belonged to this union for over 50 years. He met my mother in the YCL and they married in 1940, just before my father was called up to the RAF. She tells the story of a youth hostelling trip they made to North Wales before their marriage, which gave her a foretaste of the future.

> *We had to take our own pots and pans because, he said, ' you don't buy the food at the youth hostel, we have to cook our own food'. He said, "I'll carry the pots and pans" - and I carried the* Selected Works of Lenin *in my rucksack. I thought, because he said it and he was so much older than I was, it must be all right. In fact the people going from hostel to hostel christened me 'the bloodhound' because my nose was so close to the ground - these books were so heavy, I had to walk bent double all the way.*

The war period was the biggest influence on their lives, particularly as the city was subject to heavy bombing. In an interview taped by my sister, my mother described the frightening pattern of nightly air raids: one night she stayed overnight with her mother and when she returned to her flat it was 'not there', having been reduced to rubble. The YCL urged everyone to join the war effort and, as she put it, 'If the YCL said jump I jumped.' In the factory she made parts for Spitfires in 12 hour shifts, receiving £7 a week compared to the £2.50 paid in the previous office job. 'We would start at 7pm in the evening and at 12 there would be roast dinner and a cabaret to keep the workers happy,' she said. There was incessant bombing, that was so bad that 'at one point people were saying they could not take much more of it.' They got used to rationing, with two ounces of meat a week, no fruit and vegetables, and queues for most essentials.

Later she trained as a factory inspector and then left work when she became pregnant. After the war she was active in the CP and served for two years on the national executive. She wrote, 'I was specially trained as a public speaker by our beloved Harry Pollitt and spoke at hundreds of meetings large and small. I was in charge of political work among women for many years and was given the responsibility of organising opposition to the Korean War among the women in Liverpool.' When her three children were older, she became a teacher but still remained active in the CP. For her it was a lifetime commitment and she had a gut instinct that the party was right. She was unshaken by the Cold War and the Soviet invasion of Hungary, retaining a certainty that occasionally seemed dogmatic.

My father had been an electrician in the RAF and, after the war, carried on that trade at Cammel Lairds shipyard at Birkenhead, and with other electrical firms. He then qualified as an accountant and practised on his own, apart from a period when he ran a small tailor's shop in Liverpool, inherited from his father. He once said that some people are born rebels, and 'I think I was a born anarchist'. His politics put him at odds with his family and they came to regard him as 'a shadowy figure'. This estrangement lasted for many years and he appeared to feel uncomfortable about his parents' suburban lifestyle.

He was drawn to Marxist ideas and said that 'it was a bit like a drug, once you got Marx into your system it was difficult to get it out'. He read a book on Lenin by Ralph Fox and saw Russia as the model for the future development of all modern societies. Having read the theory, Russia appeared to be putting it into practice; it was only later he realised there could be other paths to socialism. His father was a rather intimidating figure and my father once said that 'the way I saw him was probably the way you saw me, or didn't see me! Men went to their businesses, women stayed at home and looked after the children'. While also loyal to the party, he had an intellectual commitment which was capable of criticising policy, particularly in later years when he saw the pro-Soviet hardline faction of the CP as backward-looking.

In 1960 he took a job as accountant at the *Daily Worker*, which subsequently became the *Morning Star*. This was a conscious decision to work 'in the movement' and, while it gave him a measure of security, the job was not well paid and carried no pension entitlement. It is fair to say that my father had total commitment to the CP and the trade union movement which overrode everything else. Most evenings were spent at meetings and there were always demonstrations and other activities at weekends. At the time I don't believe that that was as much an issue between my parents as the financial problems stemming from lack of a reasonably-paid job. Such a traditional concern could be sacrificed to the needs of the party and often we struggled to make ends meet until my mother became a qualified teacher. My mother undoubtedly resented this and later in life she felt that the family paid too high a price for my father's CP commitment.

On the other hand we benefited from the atmosphere of debate and discussion in the family and were encouraged to express our opinions. We felt acutely what was going on around us, such as the perceived threat of nuclear war, which made the film *The War Game* seem like a portent of things to come. With the parades, festivals and CP socials there were definite advantages to a communist upbringing.

LOOKING BACK

My own background, and that of my sister and brother, contains many of the CP rituals that other people refer to in the interviews that follow. There were May Day marches through Liverpool, coach trips to Labour Party conferences to lobby for nuclear disarmament, CP socials, and a summer trip to Czechoslovakia, staying at a youth pioneer camp. I marched with the Woodcraft Folk through the suburbs of the south east to huge CND rallies in London, and joined the YCL, selling *Challenge* magazine to Saturday morning shoppers.

My early life can be divided into two phases, rather in the way that Hywel Francis describes his. The CP in Liverpool, with its background in the docks and industry around Merseyside, was a fairly tight-knit society in which people and families knew each other well. Within the CP, class barriers did fall down so I met working-class families in a way I probably otherwise would not have done. I grew up seeing other 'comrades' at meetings, May Day rallies and at the CP bookshop, and playing with their children. For several years we all went on summer holidays to a place called Wortley Hall in Yorkshire, which was a small stately home owned by the TUC. The parents held political education meetings while we explored the grounds.

Liverpool had its own Unity Theatre group in which the works of Bertold Brecht were popularised and performed. At school I think I inherited a certain intellectual arrogance about the state of the world. I knew that in Britain certain wrongs had to be righted and that abroad Russia, when it came down to it, was on the side of 'the workers', which was the only side to be on. There were a few other CP kids and we knew we were all in a private conspiracy together, although we had other friends.

I went to primary and then grammar school, before the second phase occured, when we left Liverpool to move to London because my father started his job at the *Daily Worker*. At the time I did not understand why my family had to move and we had to leave our friends and social networks behind. Retrospectively, I see it was a traumatic change for a 12 year old boy to be placed in a completely different environment; certainly my mother suffered from the loss of close party friends. I found it hard to settle at school and I can remember being bullied in the school yard, but I did make it to the sixth form and later university.

The backcloth to this period of my life was coloured by political/historical events such as the Cuban Missile Crisis of 1962, CND and Ban the Bomb, the return of the 1964 Labour government, the Vietnam War, the French student riots of 1968, the Soviet invasion of Czechoslovakia, and later the growth of opposition movements in Eastern Europe such as Solidarity. Increasingly, the trend was moving away from seeing the USSR as the main inspiration for socialist ideas. I identified more with the liberation movements of the Third World, in places like Zimbabwe and Mozambique. I wanted to see for myself whether a kind of African socialism was possible, and I travelled to Tanzania in 1975, encouraged by the image of Julius Nyerere as *Mwalimu*, the teacher.

Yet the links with Russia remained profound, with trips to see Soviet films, the Bolshoi Ballet, the Moscow State Circus and the Red Army Choir, and an interest in Soviet magazines. When my mother needed medical treatment, the party paid for her to go to Moscow to stay in a sanitorium. The connection was brought home to me in the summer of 1968 when I found myself working for the Russian Shop at the Russian Exhibition in Earls Court. One morning I walked the gauntlet of demonstrators protesting at the Soviet tanks rumbling into Czechoslovakia to crush the Prague Spring. Inside there was a strange atmosphere, with protesters rushing around shouting at us; one log cabin was set on fire. I suddenly felt uneasily that I was in the wrong place. I stopped going after that.

Both my parents stood as CP candidates for local elections in Liverpool and London, which marked us out from the crowd in a visible way. I wrote later:

> *Sometimes I went canvassing with Dad when he was standing as a party candidate in our local area. I just tagged alongside him, always running to keep up, as he went from door to door explaining something about the bomb or peace or things like that. People always listened to him, although some got angry and banged the door shut.*
>
> *Dad got very nervous as the election date came near, talking about the number of votes he would get and hoping to increase it from the 200 odd he or Mum or anyone else got when they stood for the CP. On the night of the count, we went to bed, but were woken up by lots of shouts and noise. We rushed to the top of the stairs and they were all shouting something about 303, 303 all the time, as though they had won. The next day I realised the Labour candidate won with over 5000. I could never understand how everyone got so worked up about 300 votes.*

As I grew up I had this strong sense that my politics made me different from other young people, and a related sense that I was an outsider, apart from the mainstream. I became consumed by the idea that I wanted to 'belong', be accepted, and I am sure this has some roots in a Jewish background. I did have a barmitzvah when I was 14, a fact that has always slightly puzzled me since my parents were confirmed atheists and completely suspicious of religion or church attendance. It was explained at the time as a duty in deference to my father's mother who was an active Zionist, which sounds like my CP father being able to have his Jewish cake and also eating it. I was confused and somewhat embarassed by the whole event. For several weeks my parents believed I was at the synagogue immersing myself in the Sabbath service and preparing myself for the 'coming-of-age' ceremony, when in fact I was walking the streets just wishing the whole thing could be over with.

Within my family there was a clear demarcation in terms of domestic responsibility. My father believed that his clear role was his political work, and my mother's was to keep up the house and do most of the child-rearing. In the years before the feminist movement challenged ingrained atttitudes, CP men simply did not see domestic work or even family activities as a priority, compared to the historic task of 'building the movement' and 'working with other progressive forces'. This is not to say that my father did not love his children, but in the grand scheme of things socialism and communism came first. My mother initially accepted this division of labour, but later it angered her and was a cause of tension in the family. Because we, as children, were in the house more, she conveyed these feelings to us and we perhaps realised at first hand the personal inconsistencies that come when people dedicate their lives to a universal and all-encompassing ideal.

While our house was frequently full of debate and discussion, and sometimes CP meetings were held there, it could be a frustrating experience trying to question certain policies. You would be told that you did not understand the issue because 'it was a class question' or you would be told you were being 'emotional' and not 'rational' about a subject. For instance, I was told I could not appreciate what the enemies of the Soviet Union had done and wanted to do in the future, against which any weaknesses of its system paled into insignificance. The act of political discussion itself could be an exhausting and ultimately unsatisfactory experience.

While I was at university my feelings about my upbringing came to a head. I re-appraised my political heritage and decided that it all had to be re-evaluated; nothing could be taken on trust any more. It was a kind of personal crisis in which the CP seemed to have little to offer, and to be, in a general and rather fuzzy sense, simply out of date.

It seemed to me that political thought had to be re-invented, and while I did study Marxist ideas, I found anthropology and sociology much more refreshing. After university I went into street theatre, perhaps feeling that the old politics of marches and speeches was worn out, and did some lecturing before becoming a journalist.

Although I never joined the CP, I was somehow tied to it by a political umbilical cord which, in retrospect, made it difficult to forge my own political identity. When it came to finding a job in 1975 when I was unemployed, it seemed easier to accept an offer from the *Morning Star* than to try alternative ways of building a career, as a freelance journalist or working on another paper. I did believe in the idea of a mass left-wing daily and hoped the *Star* could become that, but perhaps also I instinctively felt my parents would approve.

At the paper I came up against CP members who wanted to maintain a rigid control over the paper as a party organ rather than expand the circulation on a wider basis. Naively I thought I could help to change attitudes; but I was wrong and I was also caught in the bitter CP split in which the paper became the propaganda tool of one faction. It was not a pleasant experience and left me wary of ideological commitment.

My father spent his formative years in intense political activity, supporting the Republicans in Spain and the unemployed in Britain, while my mother was out working; but I was less inspired by politics and I suppose more 'irresponsible'. The 'sex, drugs and rock and roll' era of the 1960s and 1970s, during which I went to university, seemed to make it acceptable. Politics appeared to be merely one branch of a cultural explosion - so whether it was street theatre productions mocking racist police behaviour, or Bob Marley concerts, I felt that that was 'where it was at' in terms of being anti-establishment. Since our parents held values and moral attitudes formed in the 1930s and 1940s, they were unlikely to share my views.

I was also sympathetic to some Trotsykist ideas, and organisations like the International Marxist Group, which for CP members was such a betrayal that it could not be talked about in polite company. This was reflected in the hierarchy which obtained on my father's bookshelf: Lenin on top, followed by Marx, Engels, a few Stalin tomes, then Mao Tse-Tung, with Trotsky discreetly tucked away at the bottom. When I confessed to my mum that I was reading a biography of Trotsky by Deutscher, she almost spat out the words, 'not that dirty Trot?' The origins of such bitterness date way back to the 1920s, but it doesn't change the fact that the CP seemed incapable of having a dialogue with ideas different to its own; looking back this seems crazy when there were young people ready to confront the status quo in society.

Part of my growing dissent with the CP was the feeling that it failed to locate the individual as an entity, as opposed to the collective, the class, the 'movement'. Marxism was supposed to enable individual human beings to achieve their full potential as individuals, but in practice individual rights were given a much lower priority and could always be sacrificed to the needs of the party or the state. If communist parties in Eastern Europe had sought to reform their over-centralised monolithic states in the 1950s, history might have told a different story.

This whole debate crystallised in the Prague Spring, which for many younger socialists was the most exciting development to occur in their lifetime, offering, as it seemed to do, an integration of human rights with socialist planning. This was too dangerous for those who believed that 'freedom of expression' was a luxury no socialist state could afford.

One day my mother received some Soviet literature from my uncle in the GDR, explaining why the Czech Communist Party was being led astray by West German agent provocateurs whose real aim was to bring the Czech Republic back into the capitalist fold. There were intriguing pictures of western tourists in Prague, West German military manouevres and one of a couple kissing in a park, which was meant to illustrate the decline into decadence. CP puritanism was rearing its head yet again. My mum didn't say much but I knew she believed it.

As far as I was concerned, the snuffing out of that creativity among Czech socialists and communists was the deathknell of modern communism. The British CP might have ended in 1991 but enthusiasm for its principles probably died with the Soviet tanks that rolled into Prague in 1968.

INTERVIEWS

NON-STOP PARTY

JACKIE KAY / ALEXEI SAYLE

JACKIE KAY was born in Scotland in 1961 and has made a name as a poet dealing with issues of sexuality and feminism, Scottishness, and being black and working-class. Her first collection of poetry, The Adoption Papers, *which describes her adoption and upbringing by CP parents, won several awards, including a Scottish Arts Council Book Award. She also writes for TV and theatre and now lives in London.*

ONE BIG PARTY

The first thing I remember is getting dressed up to go to events. I might be wearing a navy dress with a white collar and new shoes or get a bright red trouser suit with red bell bottoms. I remember one time going to a *Morning Star* bazaar, and Jack Ashton, who was secretary of the Scottish CP, coming up to me and saying 'nice colour, comrade'. I was wearing this bright red bell bottom trouser suit - it was a strange mixture of fashion and politics. My mum said, 'Red always suits you.'

I went to miners' galas in Edinburgh, from a very young age. We would go down the Royal Mile and always pass the place where all these old people would be wheeled out to watch the march. There was an old people's home there, and they would all wave, and I always thought I was doing something that was cheering.

It felt festive; most of my early memories of political experiences were very joyous and festive, like one big extended party: going through to Edinburgh with all the floats and people singing and dancing, and the miners' beauty queen contest! The whole calendar was full of events. January had Burns' Supper and I was taken to them from a very early age. The haggis, neeps and potatoes was almost a communist supper.

I did feel myself as part of a community of like-minded people. From early on I was aware that the Communist Party was like the *Secret Seven*. On a Saturday we went and got our meat from the party butcher; if anything went wrong with the plumbing the party plumber would come and do it; or if we had a new carpet fitted the party carpetter would come; if we wanted new cupboards the party carpenter would come. There was an endless series of people and it was something you didn't really question, all you knew was you were getting things cheap. The party butcher always gave us four slices of slicing or square sausage free, and we would get a lump of steak every Saturday much cheaper because otherwise we wouldn't have been able to afford it.

My dad worked full-time for the Communist Party and there wasn't enough money to afford things like that. His money was made up from *Morning Star* bazaars and paper sales and a lot of time there wasn't money to pay him. If they didn't have any money he didn't get paid.

Another early experience, around seven, was going from door to door with my dad when he was standing in elections in the Gorbals. I remember going up to this woman's door - to most of the people I would say 'vote for my dad', it was almost American in a way, and most people would think I was very cute - but this particular woman said the Communists were the devils and did I know what they represented and how disgusting sending a child around, and she started to create, and my dad came and rushed me away.

May was May Day and we would always have this walk in Victoria Park in Glasgow and assemble at George Square. Each year you would see the same groups of people, and it would be exciting to see them - you would see them at other events, so there was this bunch of friends of my parents. They would assemble under different banners and they would be dressed up. At the end there would be speeches which I always thought were quite boring. Then we would go to Jessie Clarke's. She was a CP member and like an aunt. She was a cook and would make the most lavish meals, so there would be 20 or 30 people in her garden. Her husband was head of Equity, the actors' union, so there would often be actors there - the whole thing had a glamorous feel to it.

In the summer was the miners gala and at Christmas was the *Morning Star* bazaar, and at other times there were various CND marches, anti-apartheid marches or marches in support of Upper Clyde Shipbuilders. Then there were lots of rallies where you would meet at a big hall and people would speak. I remember I used to run up and down with my dad, and people would say, 'There's John Kay,' and I would feel a real surge of pride in my father who was almost in control of the world, or so it seemed to me. It is really funny now when you look back and see what a small party it was - it seemed to have a huge influence and he seemed to know a tremendous amount of people.

My mum was in the party too. I remember at one such party event she got up and read some poems, and I remember being really proud of her for getting up and doing something because she often did background organising. She was secretary of Scottish CND for a number of years, so she went to the World Peace Festival in Russia and was away for a month, and my dad looked after us. She came back with Russian toys and dolls.

MEN BEHAVING BADLY

I was very conscious that I was different. I remember writing an essay when I was seven on 'what your dad does'; I said, 'My dad is a party man, he organises parties.' And all the kids in the class were saying, 'Does he really,' and I said, 'Yes,' although I am not sure if I really believed that he went around organising people's birthday parties. But it seemed to me to be a nice idea and in a way it was like a non-stop party.

But I also learnt from an early age to be secretive about my father's work, and my mum said to judge who to say it to. My mum was quite secretive about my dad being a Communist to certain people at school and in our area, because we lived in quite a middle-class part of Glasgow. When we came home in our car, which had election posters saying 'vote John Kay, Communist' plastered all over it, I always felt self-conscious arriving back to this suburban street. My mum said that if some people asked what your dad did and you didn't like them, to say he was a draughtsman, because that's what he was by training. So to some people I said he was a draughtsman and to other people a CP organiser. I did learn that; children do learn who to say it to, the same as if you are a child of a gay person, you learn who it is OK to say it to and who not. I think my son already knows to do that and he is only six. They learn things like that pretty quickly.

We had party socials in the house. We had loads of those, where people came round and paid a fiver at the door to make money for the party and have a good time. It would be, 'Whose turn is it for the song?' and everybody had certain songs they sang over and over again and certain ways of singing. I wrote a poem about that called 'Watching People Sing', which was about a party social; I used to spend my whole time watching people's mouths, and how affected and theatrical everybody was. This was their performance spot and their moment.

We went on Scottish trade unionists' trips abroad, and we went to Romania three years running, and Yugoslavia. There used to be about 80 people on them. We stayed in the same hotels in a resort on the Black Sea. Each year tragedy struck, which is why I remember them. One year one of the Communists got drowned. The red flag was up (the danger flag not the Communist flag) but he went in anyway, drunk, and hit his head against a rock. My dad and another man jumped in to try and save him. I wrote a children's poem about that called 'The Black Sea'. Another year someone died in their room, and another year two Romanian boys locked me in this shop, trying to attack me and a friend of mine for which they got two years' hard labour. So these party holidays seemed very dramatic.

I think the party for my dad did come before his wife, his family and everything really. He spent much more time with the party doing party things than he spent with his wife or family. I did feel a huge amount of resentment towards him for that for many years, and at the time. He worked every single weekday and would often be in at 11 at night, and back there again at nine in the morning. And he would work weekends, so you would be lucky if on a Sunday he would be finished at two or three. Saturday he often worked until five or later and often he'd have weekend schools away.

Even on one holiday, to the Isle of Mull on the west coast of Scotland, I remember him being called back because we were in the middle of some shipbuilding crisis and he went back to Glasgow, then back to join us. It is ridiculous, now I think about it, to break off a holiday to do that sort of thing.

Men seem to have trouble combining the demands of a family with the demands of work. If that 'work' is going to improve the whole world in their eyes, then letting their families down has some justification. The good of the world is a tall order for a small working man.

I used to think, why can't they work it out better. Most women manage to have beliefs and yet still keep up commitments that are personal. Men with beliefs find it harder to do that; men find complexity more difficult to manage and they can't juggle two different things at once. Often when my dad was at home he spent a lot of time being fanatical about football and watching sports, so you would ask something and he would go, 'Shhh'. He's not into all that now, I think he's a bit ashamed of it. My dad's a feminist now and he's changed quite a lot.

SACRIFICE FOR WHAT?

So my dad gave all of his life, from when I was four until very recently, nearly 30 years of solid working, and no pension, no nothing. And he didn't take out his own insurance policy. I think the party was irresponsible.

To look after their own was seen as being selfish; but in actual fact there is a huge irony. You have all these workers' rights, and my dad going into unions and helping miners and train drivers to get their big cars, while all the time he is driving around in this beaten up old thing which breaks down on motorways. It seems crazy that he was a worker himself and worked very hard, and he ought to have had workers' rights. I used to say this to him when I was 16 or 17: 'where's your rights?'

There was an element of people thinking you had to make a sacrifice, if you believed in something hard enough the only way you could prove how much you believed in it was to make a sacrifice; That idea is very religious in a way, like Jesus Christ, and it runs through our moral teaching. There is an attitude that you cannot be serious unless you suffer, and it seems to me to be a silly attitude. If challenged about not having these things yourself as a Communist you say, 'Oh, that's different because I am fighting for other people to get these things.' My dad loved his work, loved going to meetings and talking at factory gates. He loved engaging with political concepts and ideas, and still does. He wasn't and still isn't interested in material things. He's just turned 70 and I asked him what he wanted for his 70th birthday and he didn't want anything, he wasn't interested. In that sense he is a true Communist and a true idealist. Material things don't bother him.

On the Soviet Union, my dad always was critical of them. When the party split, his friend Alex Clarke went on the pro-Soviet side, and it was split down the middle; so a lot of people I had grown up with weren't friends any more, and that was very strange and sad. He never criticised it properly in the way you criticise fascism, he would always make excuses and make justifications as to why they behaved as they did. Any criticisms he would make he made in private, so the criticisms were secret and part of the secret society. You'd never speak to anyone who was anti-communist and tell them you criticised the Soviet Union: you had a very loyal sense about what you said in public, which was another mistake.

CP LOVE AFFAIR

There is always a blind spot if you love something. People's relationship with the Communist Party was a kind of love affair. People would get tearful talking about their beliefs and there was this fierce, passionate language of protest. It was like a mother's love for a child and a lover's love for a lover. Often, in those kinds of relationships, love is blind: you cannot be critical of the thing you love, because to be critical of it is somehow to hurt it or destroy it. People don't realise that if the mother is able to criticise her child, that child will grow up a better child than the child who is not criticised. They don't realise that, had they spent more time criticising their child, it might have survived. Instead their child got killed or put in prison and locked up.

Also, because of the McCarthy period, there was a fierce paranoia and hatred of communists in the media, with the 'reds under the beds' scare and people being hounded and hunted down; so people felt if they criticised it would be misinterpreted as being the same as McCarthyite criticism. It is like the question of what you do when a black person is seen to behave abominably - how do you criticise that without being seen to be racist? It is a delicate kind of situation and people get morally confused. People have to decide their priorities and speak out, no matter what it might look like to McCarthy in America or Stalin in Russia, but it is very difficult.

Every lobby, whether feminist or anti-racist, has been snookered by that one thing, not being able to criticise enough your own concepts. There is a fear of becoming the enemy within and going over to the other side and betraying your love, which is very deep. The party was like a family, and when there were splinters going off that was like parts of your family getting lost and going missing, like a child gone missing.

Scottish Communists didn't identify with England; even with English party members, they would be criticised for thinking London was the centre of the universe. The London party was thought to be very chauvinistic. Scottish members would say, 'do they realise we are getting on a bus and travelling right down for 12 hours'. The English people, although they were part of the same family, were more like strange cousins who spoke with different accents.

At first my dad thought feminism was very divisive, like all people did in the 1970s. Then he embraced feminism and he is much more conscious of gay issues, and he has kept changing, as my mum has. They have always been open to changing their views, they have never been didactic or dictatorial. When I was 14 I joined the YCL and my dad ran up and down the living room shouting, 'Helen, she's taken a party card'. It was my decision to join, although my brother was furious with me and said I was only doing it because my mum and dad wanted it. My brother was also black and also adopted. He is older than me. He was annoyed and said he was going to vote Tory and thought I was too young. I joined because I had similar beliefs to them. An example was that I thought apartheid was wrong and I found it very stimulating when I used to go to meetings and listen to ideas about apartheid, poverty or even women's rights, which they dipped into. Me and my friend Alistair joined at the same time, and left at 16 because they were not opening up, and whenever we asked questions about, for instance, gay sexuality, they would close right down and not want to discuss it and we decided they were not open enough for us.

In some ways joining might have been to get parental approval, but it didn't feel like that at the time. A lot of the time you find getting approval from political parents is different from getting approval from parents who are not. With them I imagine you get approval by cutting the grass or washing the car; for the political child the way to get approval is to have good beliefs and have a good mind. I used to argue and both my parents used to sit back spellbound and admiring. I used to write all these poems about apartheid, God, and poverty in the Gorbals. My first poem was published in the *Morning Star* when I was 12. It was about poverty - all that early poetry was political. I'd send it off to different literary magazines and they'd send it back saying, 'There isn't enough of you in this. It's very good but too polemical.'

I found the YCL conferences in London very exciting. I came down on a bus with other people. Eventually I didn't feel there was a place for me, I felt it was excluding me and didn't recognise my experience.

I was 17 when I first decided I was a lesbian but we didn't discuss it in the family, and haven't for a long time. We haven't discussed it in a 'Let's sit down and talk about it' approach; it was more my dad asking if I'd seen something on the telly, sneaking it in as a way of acknowledging it. Scottish people have difficulty talking about issues of sexuality, the whole country is very uptight about sex to an incredible degree. My parents are now very accepting of my life and my partner.

ON THE MARGINS

When I was brought up, I was given certain values and beliefs that were very nourishing and very good for me, and I incorporated them into my whole personality; they have never left me and never will because they are in my blood. I have taken them from my environment, almost like a mural or collage that you put together. Angela Davis being imprisoned in the 1970s - I was very upset about that and I identified with her because I thought I looked like her. I had 'Free Angela Davis' posters on the walls of my bedroom, not Donny Osmond or David Cassidy. I was almost in love with her in a way, she was my first great heroine. The blues women were my other heroines because my dad loved blues and jazz and I was aware of the hardships they had gone through in America.

I still believe in equality and in being fair to people, it's my moral code and way of looking at things. If something happens in the street I have to intervene and defend people. I have this lifelong sympathy with people who are outsiders, on the margins, who are not included in mainstream society.

The borders are where it happens; the borders are where there is the most activity and we can see that right around the world. If you look at war, it is there, if you look at sexuality, things happen on the borders. Now I use this way of looking at the world in everything that I write and it informs the characters I create, the poetry I create and the plays I create.

I wrote a play about two gay men in a small mining town in Scotland, a miner and a barber who had an affair with each other; the miner was a married man. This play was on last year and toured round small communities in Scotland, and was also at the Edinburgh Festival and got an award. The thing people talked about was this standard macho man being gay. I am interested in looking at complexity. I was brought up with this great reverence for miners. My grandfather was a miner and he was buried alive twice. I wrote about a miner who was gay because my life, being Scottish and black and brought up in a Communist Party household and being a lesbian, is complicated. It is all about identity, and one bit of an identity meeting another. Sometimes people just look at Scottish issues, or women's issues or black issues and they don't look at things from an integrated view.

I am not sacrificing everything. I spend a lot of time with my child. I spend a lot of time thinking and I spend time on things that give me pleasure. I am much more hedonistic than my father,

I go to saunas, I go to homeopaths; although some things I have guilt about because I feel we live in times that are apathetic, and my only contribution to politics is my writing. I am not active in the way I used to be. Before, I would have been out in the streets campaigning about someone like Joy Gardner.

It is not just me that is not doing it anymore. It is Thatcherism that has killed it off, but it is very sad that we are all politically active in a different way and a lot of it is inside our own heads; it is very insular, very inward-looking and not outward. The politics of my childhood were all outward: you were out on the streets, out on marches, out in parks, out doing things. Now the politics of my early 30s are very inward and that I regret. My writing is a solitary activity. I don't even write with other people.

It has influenced the way I bring up my son. I want to give him some of the values I was given, I want to teach him that everyone has not got the same money and there are poor people in the world. He is always looking at books and asking 'Why are there no black people in these books?'; and, with adverts, saying 'Do black people not use washing powder?' - so he has got that already. It pleases me enormously. When he wants to take a book into school, he wants to take one that makes noises when you press the buttons. I say, 'Why don't you take a proper book in?', and he says, 'Look, the book time is our time so if I want to take in a book that gives the other children a bit of a laugh and a bit of fun then that is up to me. All day long we are taught what the teachers want to teach us, we never have our own choice about what we learn.' So I have to say, 'Fair enough.' Six years old and he has a tremendous sense of being able to weigh up concepts.

LOSING YOUR GOD

I think faith in communism was a kind of religion. They wouldn't like to compare it with religion because religious people can be very cruel and very hypocritical; and they are neither cruel nor hypocritical, so it is not like religion in the sense of going to the church on Sunday and doing one thing and then doing another thing 'behind God's back' as it were. But it is like religion in terms of intensity of belief, and now, with the break-up of the Communist Party, the terrible loss and the lack of faith, it is like losing your God, and people are all over the place.

I see Communists dazed and befuddled and surprised at having lost their way, the way that people look after someone has died, grief-struck and in shock, and trying to soldier on and be in the Democratic Left and continue to do things. But the heart has gone, something very vital and hugely important. The core and kernel of their belief system has gone and that is like losing your God. It is a terrible thing to happen and terribly sad. It is not a loss for our generation in the same way but I do feel it is very sad on my parents' behalf.

If you compare the Communist Party to a family, I do feel like I'm the grandchild and my parents had such and such a story and this has gone and has been handed down to me like a family jewel. It is like the generational pattern of repeating a political cycle which cannot happen in the same way, now that the CP has died. Perhaps in 20 years time or 50 years a new Communist Party will be born, but it has come to the end of its cycle; so something new needs to happen and it will take time to see if it's a good thing or a bad thing. But at the moment it is suspended time, it is limbo.

ALEXEI SAYLE is a Liverpool-born comic, TV personality and writer. His father was active in the CP and rail union on Merseyside. He studied at Chelsea School of Art and made his name as a compere at the Comedy Store in London in the early 1980s. He was a member of a Maoist group for several years.

TAKEN FOR A RIDE

It always seemed to be a constant that my parents were political. I can remember giving smart-arse answers in primary school to questions. Teachers would say we should thank God for milk and I would say 'No, it comes from the Milk Marketing Board or from cows'. I can't really remember a time when I wasn't political.

My parents must have joined the party after the war, they were in Unity Theatre and socialist rambling clubs. My dad was active in the trade unions and the Labour Party, while my mum had been in trade unions in the garment industry and been organising strikes. When I was young I used to go on marches. There were always meetings at our house, I can remember the front room filled with smoke and large men having meetings and conspiring, I suppose. I remember we used to get the *Daily Worker* and there was this French cartoon called *Pif* which was translated from *L'Humanité*, the French CP paper; I suspect it wasn't that funny in French and it certainly wasn't funny when translated into English.

My mother didn't work when I was young. My father was a guard on the railways and was union secretary in Merseyside and North Wales district. We used to go to a lot of meetings and we went to annual conferences; we might stay for two weeks if it was Bridlington or Scarborough or Southport. He got a free pass which entitled us to ride free on all the council amenities wherever the conference was, so you got free deckchairs in Scarborough or free train rides. I don't remember my dad being around that much with all his union work; he was either working shifts or at meetings. I was born in 1952 and I was an only child.

I did mix with party friends. Later at school my best friend was Cliff Cocker, whose mother was active in the CP. We were proud as a family of being different, it was almost fostered in us.

We were superior, more bohemian - we used to have salad sometimes for our Sunday dinner. It was as if we didn't need to conform to ideas of petty one-upmanship that the rest of the street did. I can remember buying East German wooden toys at the *Daily Worker* Christmas bazaar.

There was this peace thread connected to this rapacious militarism, they always seemed to excuse aggressive behaviour in the Russians. We were taught to sneer at people who left in 1956 over Hungary, like our doctor, he was considered a wimp in our house for doing that. I used to bring a Marxist analysis to bear at school, I think it was just showing off really. I was occasionally involved in debates about the Royal Family and I would always take a left-wing line. I was in CND and went on their demos; Pat Arrowsmith used to live around the corner from us and I can remember buying badges off her and occasionally selling badges in the school yard.

I was never interested in organisations, I was only interested in the pose really, I never had a position all the time I was involved in politics. I joined the YCL when I was about 14. It was an unthinking thing that you joined them, I just thought I would go along, like a social thing. I seem to remember the bloke who ran it was about 40; there was a lot of that dubious stuff about being far too old.

We went abroad for our holidays because we went to Eastern Europe while everybody else was going to Blackpool. The first year - I can't remember how old I was - my parents went to Czechoslovakia for a camping holiday and there was this terrible campsite. My dad walked off and found the local trade union headquarters and introduced himself as a fraternal comrade so they fixed everything, they got us moved into a hotel. Then he made contact with people in the Czechoslovak politburo and started organising delegations of holidays for railwaymen. They came over to visit us a few times.

We went to Czechoslovakia about four times. We travelled free by train in the UK and abroad because all railwaymen got free travel right up to the Russian border. You got something like six trips a year. They were all right. We would go around tractor factories, we felt superior because we were going abroad. My parents, before they were married, went to Brittany - almost unheard of for working-class people to do that; and before that they used to go on communal holidays. They would take a villa in Italy with other people before they were married, people from Unity Theatre. They used to put on plays like Arnold Wesker. They had always gone abroad every year, they just switched the focus to Eastern Europe.

There were a lot of other CP families around, and there was a certain amount of snobbery involved, an implication that we were interested in the ballet etc. There was a thread of not complying with Victorian social mores, which were still running through British life then. My mother was very anti American Hollywood culture and couldn't see the value in it, she thought it was low culture. I didn't see a lot of Hollywood cinema or Saturday morning pictures.

THE PEOPLE'S BOMB

There was a strange strain of pacifism and it seemed contradictory. This was expressed when they were in CND because they thought it was all right for the Russians to have the bomb because it was the People's Bomb as opposed to the American or British bomb. They were vaguely pacifist. They didn't want us to have guns or things like that and yet they were perfectly happy with the Russians stomping all over Hungary. There was this utter reverence for the Russians: that they had invented everything, they were perfect, everything Russian was fantastic and it was all a conspiracy against them. This even extended back to pre-revolutionary Russia with the Cossacks being the best horsemen - ignoring the fact that the reason my mother's parents left Russia was because the Cossacks were chopping her head off - that didn't seem to impinge on them. I think I was always a bit sceptical. I can remember never really quite believing in it because it always seemed absurd.

My mother, who was Jewish, married a Christian, so she wasn't that close to her family. She was a fairly volatile person and had rows with a lot of people. My dad had Alzheimer's Disease when I was fairly young. They both fell out with the CP and became disillusioned with it by the early 1960s; they never left but they never went to meetings. My mother got involved in

Vietnam campaigns; although staying in the CP, she didn't get on socially or politically and didn't really like the people who were active in the party.

I did go on some CND and Vietnam marches but I never really liked demos, they all seemed like empty gestures. But empty gestures were central to the whole experience: marching pointlessly, pointlessly selling the paper and pointlessly meeting. My dad was also active in the Labour Party and he was a secret member of the CP: he stood as a Labour candidate for the council, they had this policy of entryism like Militant. I don't know whether this was before or after the war, but I've seen an election pamphlet where he was the Labour Party candidate and proposed to 'get rid of the trams'.

Very early on I saw that that kind of modernism was completely flawed in their paternalistic welfare state - I blame them for that: high rise culture seemed to spring from their paternalistic, socialist-communist view of doing things for people and knowing what was good for people. They were wholeheartedly in favour of slum clearance; but they had a real disdain for working-class culture and couldn't see what was good in it.

I was a troublemaker at school, I wouldn't wear the school uniform, had long hair and a beard. I stayed at Alsop Grammar school until I got kicked out in the middle of the sixth form after a fight with a teacher in the tuck shop. I thought generally that the school was great and I was perfectly happy there. After that I went to Southport Art School for two years, then went to Chelsea School of Art.

MAOISM AND FUN

I was always a bit sceptical about the party, I thought it a bit odd; it wasn't believable. Pretty early on it seemed absurd to be so uncritical. Once I became a Maoist I used to question things all the time with my parents, we had screaming matches and my mum used to get hysterical. My dad was quiet and phlegmatic, my mother was a person of extremes. They were very loyal to the Soviet Union, but they got pretty sick of the British party by the early 1960s. They thought it was hierarchical and faction-ridden, out of touch - all the things that it was. Later on they went to Russia on peace cruises and spent a lot of holidays there. They still defend Stalin even now, and say these things had to be done, and he was perfectly justified in what he did.

From the YCL, people like Ian Williams were in it, and they decided to become Maoists; so I split off and went along with them because they seemed like more fun. We became the Merseyside Maoists Group, I think. It wasn't a political gesture, it often isn't. Trotsky probably just fancied someone. The way you end up in something, whether a Marxist or a fascist, has got very little to do with what you believe, you're like a pinball bouncing from one to the other. We perceived Russia to be corrupt. China seemed to be a more thrilling, young country. It's like, why support Liverpool rather than Everton: it was just like football supporters.

One of the flaws in the CP was that they were very much against individual study. Marxism was handed down to you by the party theoreticians; whereas in the Maoist group you had study every week and studied the text, so I got a good grounding in Marxist theory. You never got that in the Communist Party. A lot of people were drawn to the CP because they saw the inequalities in our society but they weren't really educated, so they had people like Palme Dutt and Harry Politt who handed down the line and it was unquestioned. They trained the few selected people and the rank and file members weren't allowed to think for themselves. The Maoists had this thing that everyone studied, which was better than the CP.

The Maoist group became the Merseyside Marxist-Leninist group and affiliated itself as the Merseyside branch of the Communist Party of Britain (Marxist-Leninist). When I came down to London I joined the London branch run by ex-CP people like Reg Birch. I never got on with them because they were both much more drab and Stalinist, and more into the rhetoric. Nobody called anyone 'comrade' in Liverpool, but in London my reluctance to call anyone 'comrade' left me isolated. They were all mental really, much more mental than people in Liverpool, who were sort of normal. I only lasted a couple of years in that and just drifted away.

After I left, my mother joined the Maoist group and used to

have meetings in her house. I was out of it by then. Later, after Marx, she got into Ireland for some funny reason and became very pro-IRA, we had screaming rows about the IRA murdering people. She went from one cause to another. I am now deeply suspicious of all organised politics. I think in an abstract sense Marx's analysis of history is still right, so I call myself a Marxist in the sense that his analysis of the past is spot-on, but his predictions for the future were completely fucked-up. Who can predict the future, it's an impossible task.

I also think that the problem with politics is people; you can't say that, if your ideology is pure, things will work out. Really, the history of socialism, as with communism, has been that these theoretically good ideas have been converted into the most appalling ends and made things worse. People's psychology or group dynamics, and people's evil side, comes into play when you try and impose ideological structures on people's behaviour.

One thing you can say for capitalism is that it is organic, it grew, and to try and replace it with some thought or invented way of behaviour seems impossible and just seems to make things worse.

I see myself as left-wing but I like to read the opposition, people like PJ O'Rourke; and I am not against the contention that for those of us in western democracies these are the best countries in the world - that always seemed to be a fault of the left, which tried to pretend that revolution was around the corner and Britain was as bad as El Salvador - it's false, it's a lie and you are going to be marginalised if you go around saying it. There are terrible things that happen in this country but they're a lot less terrible than what happens anywhere outside western democracy.

The CP were utterly deluded, both about countries they looked up to like the Soviet Union and also about their own country. Mick McGahey after the miners' strike said at one point, 'We mistook mass meetings for mass support,' and I think that is very true. You would think because you got a thousand people at St George's Hall, or got 300 votes in an election, that was significant because you kept in that tight little world. It is very easy to do that, but the people outside couldn't give a toss.

The miners' strike seemed to be the last cry of communism,

but if you see the disastrous way it was run, they failed to understand anything about the way things actually were - because they didn't want to question it. Scargill was an archetypal Communist, a man who refused to look reality in the face. He is a very impressive bloke in some ways, but also completely cut off from reality. I remember Tony Benn saying we should not say 'they lost', but how do you learn if you don't admit you lost. That seemed a typical CP mentality, the whole strike, it was empty gesture politics.

CLAIMING THE FLAG

I haven't really seen work as a therapeutic exercise. Personally I was always more angry with the left than the right because at least the right are doing it. They were doing what came naturally to them, what the left were doing were people like Derek Hatton who were taking people's noblest aspirations and completely fucking them up. It makes me furious. It is tragic and disappointing, they were so stupid in so many ways, all of them, the Communists and the Trots. Take the Anti-Nazi League, they were thrilled when there was an upsurge of fascist activity in the 1980s and 1990s, they were rather pleased.

One of the things I didn't like about my mother, and I think it true of Communists in general, is how anti-British they are, often ashamed of being British. They don't like the Union Jack - the Union Jack has been incorporated by the right, why isn't it our flag? My mother said the Russians won the war, the British didn't. Stalingrad was the key to it. Nationalism is bad unless it is Russian nationalism. For a long time I despised this anti-Britishness, but it is a very strong element in the left, the obssession with Europe and the dislike of the flag. There is a brilliant PJ O'Rourke bit about it, where he goes on a cruise of the American CP to Russia, and he pins them brilliantly. This commie woman is in this airport with Aeroflot planes and she says, 'The Soviet Union, so many planes'. He pins that down, just how ashamed they are of their own country. He says the Russians on the trip are ashamed of the anti-Americanism. If you hate your own country you hate yourself, really - nobody should hate your own country - unless you're German! It doesn't mean you think Culloden or the Amritsar massacre were good ideas.

In a contradictory way my mum always drummed it into me that my dad had been shafted by the left and they had not really risen, so I always had it bashed into me that I was going to be materially successful in a way he wasn't, which turned out to be the case.

It was made clear to me I wasn't going to be encouraged to join the proletariat and I would rise above all that - there was never any question of me working for a living, as it were! I was always convinced I was going to be famous, a lot of Jews are like this; Marx probably had a Jewish mother pushing him on. I had this quiet confidence that I would be something.

After art school I was unemployed for about five years just washing dishes and doing part-time jobs. I left Chelsea art college in 1974 and I was semi-unemployed and deciding what I wanted to do. Cliff Cocker started a drama group in 1976 - we'd been in the school play together in Alsop - which was doing songs and poems of Bertold Brecht at CP functions in London, so we did that for a couple of years. We were called the Threepenny Theatre. Then the group broke up and there was me and this CP bloke called Bill Monks left, and Cliff. I had these ideas about doing some comedy so we did that for a couple of years, touring CP benefits with me and Bill performing and Cliff directing. Then Linda saw an advert for the Comedy Store and I just took a bit I'd been doing in the show and they offered me the job as compere in 1979. Cliff had also got me a job part-time teaching.

It was a kind of support, somewhere for us to play; and also a lot of my material was about that, partly about what came to be called the yuppie lifestyle - which the CP people pioneered, the 2CV and Habitat furniture - and about the CP itself, which went down very well.

All my early stuff was about having a picture of Stalin above the fireplace scoring the winning goal for Liverpool in the 1939 Cup Final, and my bed being three inches from the ceiling because underneath it were 9000 unsold copies of the *Morning Star*. No-one had ever done anything like that before. I was the first to do lifestyle piss-takes, which again was very original, and the other stuff was doing stand-up comedy about communism.

Communists were one person in a meeting and another person out of it. It always seemed to me that people would sit and believe the most appalling crap in these meetings, and then come out into the real world. It was only when they tried to take action based on what had gone on in the meetings that they got unstuck really. People lie to themselves, people aren't consistent in any way. The family was an irrelevance. I was away when I was 18 and there never a moment's thought that I wouldn't be out sharpish. I became very aware early on that there was a dissonance in the family. A lot of CP, especially the men, would use the excuse that they were saving the world to be cruel or ignore their own families, or philander and stuff like that.

The party and the struggle came first and their family came second. Not in our house, but you saw a lot of that going on, you had to be drinking and permanently pissed because you were with the proletariat. Their personal morality didn't match up to their larger aspirations. That was very clear.

ALL IN THE FAMILY

MICHAEL ROSEN / JUDE BLOOMFIELD

MICHAEL ROSEN is a well-known author of children's books and has taken his one-man show to hundreds of schools. He was brought up in a Jewish CP family in London and became active in CND and student politics at Oxford University. He was a member of left-wing theatre groups. He now presents programmes on radio about poetry and children's books.

CP KIDS

The sense that my parents were political came at me from a variety of ways. Branch meetings used to take place in our house so I have got a very early memory of groups of people turning up and coming round the house. I have a sense that my parents had a circle of friends and these were party friends. When they saw them, conversations used to take place about politics.

Then the 'lit man' used to come over with the literature, such as *Soviet Literature*, *GDR Review* and a little sheet called something like 'Germany Today'. I supposed the word 'lit' meant two things, party literature and literature literature, which overlapped with that book *Soviet Literature*.

I knew my parents were active in the National Union of Teachers and I was aware that my mother was very active in the equal pay campaign of the early 1950s. I can remember that because she used to make lots of jokes like, 'I've got my increment', and she used to say, 'I'm 3/7ths'. An agreement was negotiated by the NUT that women would get equal pay, but not straightaway, it would take seven years to implement. Each year Mum would wave this piece of paper around and go, 'I'm 4/7ths'.

Because my parents knocked around with other people in

the party who had families, there was a culture of 'CP Kids' who would then talk about the party and Russia and things like that. We would meet on social occasions. We might go over to friends or go on holiday with them; the kids would play but things would crop up to do with your parents being in the CP. From the age of five or six I was aware we were Communists.

My parents joined the YCL when they were about 16 in 1935, but on my father's mother's side of the family, their involvement in politics goes right back to the 1880s, because my father's grandfather was in the *Bund* and his mother was in the CP. My father's mother and father met in something called the Yipsels, the Young People's Socialist League, before the First World War. My parents are exactly the same age.

My father used to attend and teach at evening classes and also attended party meetings. It didn't strike me at the time that he spent an enormous amount of time on party work. I didn't feel my parents weren't there; somehow my parents were very successful in integrating family life with party life because they had a lot of party friends who they liked as people.

We went on the *Daily Worker* May Day march every year; my parents have recollections of me in a pushchair on marches with a *Daily Worker* keeping the rain off my hat. The first demonstration I have a clear memory of is the 1956 Suez demonstration. On the Monday morning after the May Day march I used to come to school with the *Daily Worker* May Day badge, and I remember when I was about nine I came to school with it and Mr Baggs, the deputy head of my primary school said, 'Oh, we're communists are we?'. I said yes and went home and reported this to my Mum, and she said, 'Look at your shoes, you haven't polished your shoes'. I suppose if you ever want to define what a Jewish communist mother is, that is it: on the one hand you could get paranoid and think, you bastards, you are checking up on our political background; but my Mum's first thought was, 'Where's your pride, you should show you are a good communist by having good polished shoes'.

I suppose my Dad, and occasionally my Mum, must have gone away to party weekends, but I don't have a clear sense of deprivation about it. The whole terms of conversation and dialogue with the world that went on in our house was influenced by the party. Culture, party and politics were all one, I can't disentangle conversations about Shakespeare from conversations about the Second World War, Cable Street, being Jewish - it is all part of the same thing somehow.

Every news programme that was listened to, there would be a running commentary from Mum and Dad going along with it. Any time I made a joke that my parents thought anti working-class in the family, my Dad would say, 'Oh, we're being anti working-class now, are we?' There were a range of political jokes; it is almost impossible for me to separate out what is culture, CP, Jewish. There was no sense of bringing up children being separate from being in the party.

UTOPIA IN THE MAKING

We had a very, very clear sense from early on that there was something different about us. We lived in an ordinary London suburb in which there were scarcely any CP-ers around - they managed to get together a little branch of about 20 people from Pinner and North Harrow - and at that time there were very few Jewish kids around.

We lived in a weird place which was a flat over a shop, whereas all my friends lived in classic 1930s semi-detached houses. It was also odd because our house was full of books, absolutely jam-packed to the ceiling with books; and our parents were teachers so that seemed strange, because most of my friends' mothers were housewives. My parents came from the East End, whereas local people had lived in the area for years; so I had 10 reasons for feeling different.

Of course this was the 1950s and the time of McCarthyism, when Communism was the greatest danger facing the western world, and I *was* one. The Portland spies who were arrested lived in Ruislip just down the road in one of these 1930s semis. If you had been in the CP in Ruislip you would have had to be in the branch my parents were in. I had an acute sense of being different, but not only for CP reasons.

In a sense I feel my parents were displaced. They left the East End; and I became aware at about 13 or 14 that we were living in the wrong place; there were loads of other people, whether Jewish or intellectuals, and they were, in a sense, in the wrong place for them. As far as ritual occasions, I remember the *Daily Worker* Bazaar in a hall in Wealdstone and we had to do things for it like my mother making a cake. My Dad may have sold the paper at work rather than street sales in Pinner - quite a nutty idea, trying sell the *Daily Worker* on the streets of Pinner!

I have a recollection that one or two friends weren't allowed to play with me and I never found out why. There was one boy who used to say, 'Would you say goodbye at the end of the road because my parents don't like the idea that I'm playing with you,' and I used to say goodbye at the end of the road.

I used to have political arguments with kids in the primary school, I have clear memories of arguing with Keith Townsend over things like the Soviet Union; about God, and saying I was an atheist. When you were in a CP family you bought the idea that this was Utopia in the making and he came from what I now look back and think was a very right-wing family. As an eight-or-nine-year old I was defending the Soviet Union and whatever strike was on, because we supported strikers. His family thought all workers were lazy bastards, and constantly striking and I would come back and say this to my parents and they would then say why people were entitled to strike, so then I would go back and argue with Keith Townsend about strikers.

There is a whole little culture around how and why do people leave the CP and do they do it secretly or are they totally open in the family. Given that my parents were very open about a lot of things, funnily enough the whole business about leaving the CP was strange and slightly secretive, there was a feeling of shiftiness. It wasn't about Hungary as far as I know. My Mum and Dad had pushed for some kind of democratisation in the London party that the party had opposed, so a group had stayed in over Hungary but left over something about London branches getting together without going through the London district organiser. I think my parents gave up on the party at that point.

As it happened they kept many of their CP friends, so, unlike many people who left over Hungary and said they weren't going to have anything more to do with those horrible CP people, they went on seeing the Kaufmans, the Flowers etc. They maintained their party friends and in a sense my father, more than my mother, never left; he went on talking about the Soviet Union and noticing the votes of the CP in France and Italy. They didn't leave the family, they left the religion.

The best analogy I always think of is with Irish Catholics: some Irish Catholics are Catholic, some aren't. You meet people, particularly from Liverpool, and they don't go to church but they are English-Irish Catholics. They know lots of Catholics and remain within a cultural mileu that has an ideological base in the Catholic Church but they are not of it although socially they are part of it; and in a sense that is what my parents were. They remained of a social mileu of party people but they had dropped some aspects of the essential catechism of the CP. They kept on with their Marxism and socialism but it wasn't CP based; they kept on with the family relationships but they weren't in the party. I remained friends with the party children, they appear in my poems, I never left the left-wing political milieu in which I would bump into CP-ers and ex-CP-ers.

'EVERYTHING IS IDEOLOGICAL'

I announced to my parents when I was 14 that I was going on the Aldermaston march; they said, 'No, you can't,' and I said, 'Yes I am, it is all right because you march with the magenta sign, which is the Harrow CND group'. I started packing my bag, and then you had the classic Jewish mother syndrome where my mother said, 'No you can't,' at the same time as stuffing chicken sandwiches in my bag. I literally walked out of the house with them saying I couldn't go. I think to be honest they were quite proud; they could see a bit of themselves in me although they thought I was too young.

I experimented a bit with the young socialists of the Labour Party. I never joined the YCL. I knew YCL-ers and went to a few meetings but I actually joined the Labour Party when I was 14 or 15 and did some election stuff, because my history teacher was Merlyn Rees, later to become Home Secretary, and he stood for Harrow East as an MP while still a teacher at our school.

If I came back with what were effectively right-wing or Tory views that was argued with. My brother now asks, 'Why was everything so ideological in our house?' What he means by that is that whether it was the way you brushed your hair, who you went out with as a girlfriend, what trousers you wore, everything appeared to be ideological. There seemed to be a rationale for a right way of doing things and a wrong way. I have less of a sense of that but I am the younger kid and he felt everything was being monitored for the right way to be. He would feel in many ways that the family was a bit intolerant.

One day Dad asked me what I was doing in history at school and I said, 'The nineteenth century. I have got to write an essay on the Chartists and the title is "Why Chartism Failed"'. 'Failed? Chartism didn't fail,' he said and asked what were the points of the charter. I went through the charter and he said, 'We've got all the points, except for annual Parliaments, so Chartism didn't fail did it?' So I go back to school the next day and I say to the teacher, 'This essay, well, Chartism didn't fail did it?'. My father intervened the whole time.

There was the time I came back from school and said, 'You once told me I didn't have to go to assembly because there is a conscience clause in the 1944 Education Act.' 'That is correct', said Dad. So I said, 'I don't want to go to assembly because I am an atheist'. He said, 'You're only saying that so you can go to school late.' 'No', I said, 'it is because I am an atheist'. So he wrote the school a letter and I handed it in to the deputy head and he said, 'Is this because you want to be late for school?' and I said, 'No, I am an atheist.' He said, 'Are you sure you don't want to go to the Jewish assembly?' My Dad always wanted to challenge things. It is legalistic, it is talmudic, it is CP, it's confrontational - and it all merges together.

My father expressed loyalty to the Soviet Union 120 per cent and they called Stalin Uncle Joe. Harry Pollitt was their hero, my father thought he was a wonderful man. I remember once going to a CP AGM and standing at the back and I could see Pollitt speaking, I must have been about seven or eight, and my father saying afterwards, 'What a fantastic speech'. There was a tremendous sense of awe and debt about Stalingrad and the millions who died. We, both as Brits and as Jews, were saved by the Russians in the war.

There were books we were given to read about Russia: one was called *Tomorrow is a New Day*, which was a Puffin book; and there was the Geoffrey Trease book *Bows against the Barons*, and *Comrades for the Charter*, early on I read *Man's Worldly Goods* by Leo Huberman, and AL Morton on *The People's History of England*. As far as Russia was concerned, it wasn't that it was paradise but they were 'doing the right thing'. If Russia was criticised then the wars of intervention were explained, the fact that there was a world conspiracy against the Soviet Union, the sense that it was anti-imperialist.

We used to get the *Observer* on Sundays and they used to read out articles by Edward Crankshaw - who they used to call Crankers - and mock him. Looking back on it, they were mocking things about the purges, about mistakes Stalin made. There was a phrase my mother used which was, 'I think Stalin must have been gaga.' Between the Russian-Nazi pact and the start of the war Stalin liquidated his chief of staff, he wiped out most of his top generals. My mother used to recount the Second World War at teatime and she said Stalin had not prepared for the war - one of the rationales the CP provided for the Russo-Nazi pact was that it enabled the Russians to get time to prepare because they knew eventually the Nazis would come.

I have a clear memory of Mum sitting there when I was eight or nine and saying, 'Stalin must have been gaga'. In a sense it was a criticism. My parents thought the pact was a clever move to buy time but Stalin didn't use it in a way he should have done to get the old tank factories going.

BAN THE BOMB

Loyalty to the world communist movement was unshakeable. It wasn't necessarily to the British CP as much as to the world communist movement. When I was at secondary school my parents were no longer in the CP but were fellow travellers. I knocked around with kids of similar background. My best friend's parents had been in the CP before the war and when I went over there his father always wanted to enter into conversations with me on the theme of: 'It was such a lovely idea but it went wrong'.

By the time I was 14 and 15 it was all around CND, and they all knew I was the only one in the class who went on the Aldermaston march. I used to get into conversations about Ban the Bomb and people used to confront me and say: 'We have got to defend ourselves.' In arguing with them I first realised the actually ludicrous position of the CP being in CND: what was the CP doing in CND when they thought the Russian bomb was OK, but the American bomb was bad and our bomb was bad? It seemed to me you either had a position where you believed in world disarmament or you didn't. What was untenable was that Britain was tagging along with the American bomb and I suppose I became a neutralist at that point. I thought it was crazy for Britain to be in either of the power blocs. Of course for CP-ers in an ideal world we would have been in the Warsaw Pact.

It came up with my parents several times and I remember saying that I was a neutralist - this was Julius Nyerere time and the possibility of third positions was beginning to emerge. Who were these people by the roadside saying Committee of 100? (the CP opposed the Committee of 100's occupation of regional seats of government) who were these anarchos, syndicalos and Trots? I started getting interested in this via CND, which was a melting pot of left-wing ideas. When I look back, I am angry because the CP position was potentially corrupting to the CND movement due to their unswerving allegiance to the Warsaw Pact. Here was the Committee of 100 exposing in great depth the extent to which Britain was implicated in this nuclear crap and here was the CP taking this 'responsible' position - I feel angry about that.

I was active in a school debating society and in the fifth and sixth form there was a group of us 'lefties' wearing CND badges.

I am 50, I was born in 1946, so in 1960-61 I went on marches and sang the songs at school. It was not only not a problem, it was upfront and with it and groovy, because it was about jazz and folk music and blues - we were the jazz and blues freaks and it was slightly risqué and bohemian, I used to go up to London and hang around the Partisan cafe in Soho, a lefty cafe, and be CNDish, wear desert boots and Levi jeans.

I was a lefty, a socialist. There was a feeling that the CP provided a left alternative to Labour, but my parents had left the CP. The Italian and French CPs were providing the alternative voice but my Mum believed 'the Russians had blown it' and thrown it all away. The Russian-Chinese split seemed to be a great loss. Looking back I can see my parents wanted to stay socialist and Marxist but they didn't have the means to analyse what was wrong with the Soviet Union in Marxist terms. They just looked at the Soviet Union as a lost opportunity.

A NEW FERMENT

I was in this limbo-land. I went to medical school when I was 18 and there was this bloke there, he had a philosophy degree and had been at the Sorbonne and studied Marxism and existentialism and was ten years older than me. He started calling me a Stalinist and I don't think at that stage I really knew the word. It was both a joke and there was an element of truth about it, because I'd never really questioned it. I was a socialist, and, all right, maybe the Soviet Union hadn't got it quite right but they were sort of socialist.

He forced me to start thinking about it all. He and his friend Ian, who was also a doctor, would grill me and talk about the show trials, the purges, effectively saying, if you were interested in being a socialist, how could it be that the kind of society going on in the Soviet Union could be held up as an example? They had been involved with the anti-Algerian war movement and had got to know the French socialist Vidal Naquet, who produced the book *Socialism ou Barbarie (Socialism or Barbarism)*, and those two came from a tradition within France of non-CP socialists, and Sartre's arguments with the CP. They had a different view of the power of the CP, which was small and seemingly irrelevant within Britain.

Suddenly this all jolted me a bit, then sat in abeyance for two or three years. I moved from Middlesex Hospital to Oxford University, and I didn't totally withdraw from politics but wasn't much involved from 1964 until 1967. I was mostly involved in theatre and journalism.

Bit by bit the events of 1968 started to hit me: I was involved with friends at Leeds where there was an occupation, then suddenly Oxford blew, to do with journalism and censorship of the student newspaper, and then about leafleting a factory. I was suddenly in another mileu of people who you could variously describe as anarchist, Trotskyist, and a lot of Third World students. All these ideas were in ferment and I was drawn in again to the anti-Vietnam war thing; I had to look much more closely at the whole position of the CP, Russian communism, the whole history of Marxism. At that point I finally shed any residual feelings that the Soviet Union was anything to do with socialism, and thought that really we had to be asking for something completely different.

I felt the nice thing about 1968 when it came along was that this felt more authentic, I was getting back to something that was politically involved but at the same dealt with some of the things that had gone wrong. The great advantage of 1968 was that it enabled you to re-evaluate all that CP stuff, but from a political perspective and not a purely emotional one.

My Dad was more bothered in 1957 with the politics of the British CP than the state of the Soviet Union. My impression was that he still felt the Soviet Union was getting there while the British CP was fucking up, and that is why he left. What you got in my teenage life was really a family in which there was strong sympathy with Eastern Europe but a feeling that the British CP had somehow screwed up. My Mum used to describe herself as an 'anarcho-Stalinist' and what she meant by that was that in her personal practice she was in favour of local democracy and anarchistic, communistic democracy, and yet within the concept of how do you take political action and take power she felt she was a Stalinist.

There was this English Trotskyist, Adam Westoby, his parents were CP friends of my parents, and he came over once and sat in our front room and slagged off the CP for about three hours. This was possibly in the late 1960s. My parents sat and listened to this until finally my mother blew and said, 'Who do you think was defending Jews in the East End of London in the 1930s? It's all very well for you to sit here in the 1960s and talk about the betrayals of the CP over the years, but for us, as Jews and socialists in the 1930s, there was no choice. The CP were the only organisation that had the power and organisation to oppose Mosley. As YCL-ers that was the only possible route to take.' Apparently, Adam had to shut up after this. I suppose one reason my Dad remembers this and passes it on to me is to say, 'Look, we weren't dishonest, corrupt swines in the CP, we were people hanging on to the idea that Jews had to be defended and to the idea of socialism for everybody'.

You could say that Jews had fought for their emancipation from the 1820s onwards in Eastern Europe, and that gave birth to Jewish labour and socialist organisations. A lot of Jews joined CPs around the world because they saw it as emancipation for people all around the world. In a sense my parents inherited that tradition and there is a coherence to that.

The whole story of the betrayal of communism and the Soviet Union is that not enough CP-ers have ever really been able to face up to what Stalin did, or face up to the simple fact that Marxism and the revolution is about changing the relations of production, and in the Soviet Union the proletariat never did take over the means of production. The CP did not analyse that and all the betrayals and the terrible slaughters and massacres, you have to go back to that simple thing.

It is not within most CP-ers' vocabulary to describe Stalin as a counter-revolutionary, but that is what he was, he was a Napoleon. He seized power and prevented any further socialist advance taking place. The full Trotskyist position is that Russia was a degenerated workers state; I took the Tony Cliff position that it was state capitalist.

As far as arguments with parents, it was unity in action - I remained united with my parents in action. For instance, when I was arrested at Grosvenor Square, who was there to get me out at 2 o'clock in the morning but my Dad - he was there. He may have thought all sorts of things about my politics, but I was doing the right thing.

BOHEMIAN RHAPSODY

If you looked at one of my parent's friends in a nearby branch, here was someone who led a constant battle with her kids and people in the Woodcraft Folk against rock music, dope, sex, drugs and rock and roll; basically - she regarded this with an absolute puritan fervour - all this was a betrayal of the working class. My parents took an opposite view, they seemed to be almost in favour of sex, drugs and rock and roll.

Both me and my brother slept with girlfriends at home from 17 onwards; my parents never questioned me about dope and worked on the principle of giving us enormous freedoms; looking back they gave me many more freedoms than I give my kids. They slept together before they were married, they went to France when they were 18. Before their marriage, my Mum ran away from home to live with my father's mother. They were the kind of CP-ers who had been affected by the Bloomsbury end of bohemian life and it was no problem for them to encompass that within their socialism. So it wasn't like the more rigid CP-ers I knew, who regarded all that as an anathema.

From the 1960s I developed a profound disrespect for any authority, academic or institutional, which said that it was the authority and therefore it had the right to rule. For me it has to justify itself intellectually and democratically. I was nearly thrown out of university, I was nearly thrown out of film school, I was thrown out of the BBC. The same applies to left politics - I don't like the way in which, within the organisations of, say, trade unions, people have these little cabals and try to win positions. I find that pretty horrid.

You try to run your personal life on principles of honesty and trust: you don't have little nasty secrets within family and personal relationships. You believe that men and women are equal and, within personal relationships, you don't have more rights simply because you are a man. On a broader scale, we live in a society that has victims that are exploited; and there is a constant sense of being in a world society, we are not narrow little Englanders.

My parents were amazingly liberal, with a tremendous sense of personal freedom, and that has passed on. With my oldest boy, when he finished school at 16 and was fed up and didn't want to go back to school, I sat down with him and he had to tell me what he wanted to do. I didn't say: right, you are now going into the sixth form to do A levels. It was for him to discover what he wanted to do.

I don't have faith in the holy family - Mum, Dad and two kids - I have faith in the idea that people who live together have to care for each other. I live in a family, and whatever set up you have in the home is like a little factory, a little collective enterprise that produces things, and jobs have to be worked out by democratic arrangement; kids have to contribute and nothing is just put on a plate for you, and you constantly remind children of this. I am more liberal than my parents in educational ambition. My parents felt education was their saviour and pressured me and my brother perhaps more than I pressure my kids. My kids are not great achievers but I feel it would be wrong to pressure them. They have got to come to terms themselves with what they want to do.

Though I am, in media terms, successful, I wasn't in any way ambitious; all the career breaks I've had were because somebody rang me up. Every time I have tried to be ambitious I have failed miserably. I was at the BBC in 1972, but I was a general trainee and the director-general Ian Trethowan was determined that, because I was a known leftie, I wouldn't get a staff job. Even when I was given staff jobs informally by a committee interviewing me, two weeks later I'd get a letter saying I hadn't got the job. This all came out in 1984 when the *Observer* showed I had been blacklisted as Communist.

At one point I wanted to be a theatre director, then a playwright, and I had a play on at the Royal Court when I was still at university. I sat in the auditorium at the Royal Court and thought, 'Why I am I saying these things to these people?' I couldn't come up with an answer. What I am more interested in is dynamic popular performance, so I joined Roland Muldoon's CAST theatre; then I joined Sidewalk Theatre, then I joined Ewan McColl's Critics Group and later we formed a breakaway group called Combine and did agitprop theatre.

I have to justify to myself what I do. I was asked to come up with an advertising jingle for Meccano and I couldn't do it. Someone said to me, 'Write something that will attract kids and say, "Meccano is the thing you've got to have"'. I don't want to enter into the cash nexus of children's toys beyond being a consumer. It would have an immediate knock-on effect on anything I would then write and would circumscribe my freedom to criticise.

I do have to say about my parents that they were lovely and wonderful people, and my Dad still is, they did wonderful things for me but they got it wrong about the Soviet Union. I would love to be able to say that round about 1946-47 they took a deep breath and said, 'Look, this is a screw-up going on, this isn't socialism', but they didn't. That is difficult for me to deal with in some respects. I went to Paris and saw the 1938 manifesto of the surrealists against the Stalin show trials, some of whom were in the CP; they were prepared to say, 'This will not do', what I have to say about my parents is that they behaved honourably with us as kids, they tried to be intellectually honest, but somewhere after 1945 they could have let go. They were very critical of things going on in life and yet suspended their critical judgement over the Soviet Union and Eastern Europe. I suppose, as far as my parents are concerned, these are errors.

JUDE BLOOMFIELD was brought up in the East End of London by Jewish CP parents and then her family moved to the Epping Forest area. She joined the YCL and became part of the Eurocommunist tendency within the CP pressing for democratic change in Eastern bloc countries.

COLD WAR COMRADES

My parents, Alte and Betty Bloomfield, were heavily involved in politics in their early years. My father was in the London East End Communist Party in the 1930s and he was part of that Jewish East End culture and anti-fascist movement. He was self-educated, very typical of a certain kind of working-class culture of the East End.

He was a shop steward and a television tester and he was also a steward on the famous Cable Street march. He knew Frank Chapple because he was in the same CP group, and my father and Phil Piratin were personal enemies, probably a case of two rather big egos clashing. My father tells this story about Piratin at some meeting passing a resolution that Comrade Bloomfield be prevented from smoking! At that time there was no campaign about smoking, he singled him out, but apparently people ignored it and carried on with the meeting.

My father must have been influential as he taught Sam Aaronovitch economics when Sam was in the YCL. He married my mother in 1947, and my mother was a communist councillor in the East End after the war. She was on Stepney council with people who were old friends, Barney Borman and Bill Carver. Years later they remained friends - they were all working-class lads who were self-educated.

I was born in 1953 and in the 1950s my father was blacklisted because of the Cold War. He lost his job and it affected him, it made him very defensive about his politics. So as I was growing up, although I imbibed radical views from the family, my parents were politically inactive. They bought the *Daily Worker* and then the *Morning Star* but, when my father's colleague came from work or called in to pick him up, my father would hide the paper. He wouldn't put up a Communist poster at election time, and I was totally contemptuous of this. I thought it was appalling that they were ashamed of their views.

When I was 11 or 12 I became politically more aware. I joined Young Oxfam because my early commitment was to do something about the Third World. I joined Young Oxfam just when it was becoming politicised and challenging Oxfam and its Tory ladies who did voluntary work. We had a campaign within Oxfam which at the time was not successful, but which subsequently has been because Oxfam has now been transformed. I worked there and campaigned on Biafra - the left had basically dumped Biafra - and I remember raising money. I wasn't exactly organised but I had a strong moral viewpoint.

We had moved out from Stepney when I was five to a place on the edge of Epping Forest called Highams Park - my parents had this idea of fresh air and green, but I hated it because it's a lethal place to grow up in as a teenager as the transport is so terrible.

At school I was very lucky that these two mates of mine who were best friends were radical politically and we set up a student's union within the school. The National Union of Students had started a school student union, and we set up a school council. I got threatened with expulsion because we campaigned to get rid of the school hats. It went from small things to being quite political. I remember one mock election when a friend of mine stood as an anarchist and got total disapproval from the headmistress. There were these two friends and I, and someone else who we tolerated because she was in the YCL, and we all joined - her mother was a Stalinist. So I wasn't totally alone in being a Communist at school.

My mother did not want me to join the party; my father acted as though he was pleased, but really what they were concerned about was that I should study, work and go to bed early. Once I started going to YCL meetings and started staying out late there were conflicts over that. I was just interested - it was a whole new world to me.

PRAGUE: HOPES AND DESPAIR

1968, the Prague Spring and the Soviet invasion of Czechoslovakia was a critical turning point. I thought it was great that it was possible to marry our beliefs about socialism with the experience of Eastern Europe to produce something more humane and closer to the aspirations we had. I was also affected by the youth culture, particularly the music.

We wore jeans, we went to free rock concerts - there was a kind of optimism in the air that everything was possible and you could transform human relationships, we weren't very individualistic. What was interesting about the group I mixed with in the YCL was that we weren't very materialistic - to be honest it was a group of working-class people who had no money. There was no pretension and people shared, we were good mates on the whole and we believed in social justice.

I had great fun. I hadn't had that before. It was this marriage of pleasure and commitment, and it was about discovering ideas and being involved in something bigger than ourselves. We went to all those free concerts and took *Challenge* along and sold it there, so we were doing our bit and having a great time. We weren't into drugs to get smashed or to get high, we had dope and it was just pleasant. My first great love in the YCL was a railway guard. One of the things I liked about the people in the YCL, which comes from my background, is that almost all my friends were working-class people who were trying to educate themselves and all ended up going to college. None have gone the conventional route, but they all went on to do things. In 1970, when I was 16, I went on one of those youth delegations to Budapest. I went with my boyfriend so it was a real holiday, but we broke up while we were there. It was a real revelation to me to get away from the family in a group of young people.

My father was opposed to the 1968 invasion of Czechoslovakia but he never thought through the implications of it. The explanation of how it had happened and why the Soviet Union became Stalinist and had the labour camps, dictatorial structures, cult of the personality, and how you could get millions of people to accept it, he never really analysed it.

My mother tore up her party card in 1967 over the Six Day War. Her first outright opposition was on Zionist grounds: that the Soviet Union backed the Arabs and Nasser was anti-semitic. She basically accepted any criticism of the Soviet Union with moral outrage but never with much analysis. That linked into what I saw as a teenager as my Mum's consumerist phase, and what I saw as her bourgeois aspirations at the time - keeping up with her family and middle-class Jews who were becoming nouveau riche. I was very contemptous about fitted cupboards and washing machines and associated all those things together. Now I see it rather differently. I rather like her family, and my mother has changed; what has become important to her as she grows older are things like provision for elderly people, mobility, public transport, friendship. Also, fifteen years of Thatcherism re-politicised her.

There has also been this process of Jewish assimilation, which I feel quite sad about. If the central European Jewish community had defined themselves as an ethnic minority they would have fought for some kind of cultural recognition within the school curriculum and retained the social basis of Jewish culture. But by a fairly normal process in the East End, of social mobility, people moved out, and they became British like any other white group, except they had a private religion that was different. That whole social culture has become dispersed or only exists around synagogues. I found that quite difficult growing up, being Jewish but nobody knowing anything about my culture.

BEING AN OUTSIDER

I felt I was different at school, very strongly. I remember this girl Shirley who was a fellow student. One day I got really mad that nobody cared about current affairs and what was going on in the world and she said, 'Maybe it just puzzles us. We just don't know how to make sense of it'. She said it really nicely, like she was admiring me, but basically she was saying that she looked at the world and it baffled her, and that was the great virtue of Marxism, that it gave you an interpretive key to reading and understanding events.

I think it does and I still think that is the great quality of Marxism as a method, so you don't feel that terrible sense of powerlessness. It was thirty years ago and I can still hear her say it. I now see that as a great strength of being part of the Communist movement. I had a very strongly developed moral sense, a sense of moral responsibility. I felt injustice was wrong and that you had to do something about it. What she made me realise was that it wasn't that she didn't have a moral sense but that she was confused and did not have an interpretive key to find her way so she tended to switch off. I had mistaken it for lack of concern.

Being Jewish you had this sense of moral responsibility, and that is why, combined with the attack on Jews in the East End and anti-fascism, it produced that particular Jewish-Communist culture. Later on, I tried to understand where communism had been strong in Britain: I realised it had been strong where it was fused not just with the working-class but with particular kinds of working-class communities - Scottish and Welsh, where there were strong occupational communities, and in the Jewish community in London. I understood that it was not enough just to be working-class, it had to be allied to some sense of oppressed nationhood or oppression as women or related to cultural identity. That fits the way I never felt English, and people said that about me at school.

At school I was made to feel different because I was very tactile and affectionate. I used to hug people and kiss them, so I was accused of being lesbian. I didn't care because it was a way of expressing affection; and later it became clear to me they had misread my culture and that was the only way they could interpret my behaviour. For me it was the way I had been brought up and you always did that - it was why I felt different and an outsider. Until fairly recently it worried me; now I am very happy to be an outsider. Right into my adult years I was always wanting to be part of the mainstream and that is why I loved being a Communist in Italy because you could be a Communist and nobody batted an eyelid.

I was always in opposition. I had an inner voice that I always listened to. There was no way I would be swung because the leader said it. I was 14 when I joined the YCL but right from the start I had a sense of what was right. I couldn't justify the Soviet invasion of Czechoslovakia. One of my earliest memories around that was being in a park in London and seeing a group of Czechs hovering round the radio and they were listening for the news. We spoke to them and they said, 'We thought they were our friends and now they've invaded us.'

The Cold War changed my parents' relationship to politics. There was the time my father had been in hospital in 1956 with a slipped disc. I was three and he was taken away to hospital as white as a sheet. Someone in the hospital bed next to him told him stories about labour camps in the Soviet Union but he didn't really believe them. Then there was the Twentieth Congress, he was morally shocked and disapproving of that, but really the Stalinist structure of thought was still there - still is in many ways. These assumptions about the party, such as prescribing what literature you could read, the sectarian attitude to anything Trotsky wrote, that kind of thing was all intact.

My father had this kind of unconscious Stalinist thinking about Kollontai and feminists, biologistic notions about sex and sexual relationships, which he would assume were obvious and progressive. The whole structure of Stalinism in terms of democratic centralism, the party having a monopoly of information and control, those elements were still intact in my father. Some of it was Leninist, somehow the party was the guarantor and it would eventually get the right line. Long after my father was critical of Stalin, he would read *Labour Monthly* and worship Palme Dutt. When I started reading *Labour Monthly* and Palme Dutt I thought it was dogmatic, assertive rubbish, without any proof. My brother and I started challenging my father about what he was reading.

At home we could always argue politically but I found my father authoritarian and dogmatic. If I disagreed with him he wouldn't listen and just respond in the normal way. He had a series of tactics. The most common one was, 'Oh, don't be stupid, you don't know what you are talking about', which was total contempt for me - although that had nothing to do with politics - and then if you threw in something that he didn't know he would always go sceptical as in, 'I don't know about that'. Because he didn't know of it and you did, there was something inherently suspicious about it.

My brother Jon, although he is four years older than me, became political after me when he went to university. In his first year he hung around the International Socialists and then joined the party. When he came home he started attacking my father for being pompous. My father would say things like, 'Well there was a man once called Charlie Marx', as if he was on first name terms with this figure and we didn't know anything about him. It was a patronising ploy. He was one of the most widely read men I have ever known, but he had that manner, like blotting paper, of uncritical absorption of everything he read.

DEMOCRATS OR CENTRALISTS?

In the 1970s my arguments were about democracy. I believed that social democracy should be expanding democratic freedoms not taking them away. It should build on and transcend the limitations of democracy, for example, you should have democracy in the workplace as well as in society. Now I believe you have to graft the liberal democratic tradition back onto the socialist tradition so that individual rights are a protection for everybody. I think that is true in terms of the universalism of rights, so it includes rights for the bourgeoisie as well. Everybody has to have guarantees of a free trial, *habeus corpus* and the whole panoply of rights.

At that time I didn't criticise democratic centralism because I believed you could arrive at an agreed majority decision democratically. It was only much later on, in the 1980s, that I came to believe that democratic centralism was a Stalinist device and one of the things that prevented the Eurocommunist project. I had a notion of what the purpose of a Communist Party was: it had to arrive at a coherent position. Now I am more aware that, unless you allow minorities to continue voicing their opinion at all times, you end up suppressing them and they can never become the majority. The way democratic centralism works, it is like an upside down pyramid that is very top heavy. Unless you allow the connection between opposition voices down below, you always have this machinery above that can prevent it being overturned. Then, it was more a question of the party being able to express all views freely and come to some decision enabling it to act in a unified way.

It was when I saw the party operating in conflict situations where I was part of the minority that I felt, why could not oppositional people get in touch with each other horizontally? That wasn't allowed and I thought, why not?

I came to see that one of the reasons Eurocommunism failed was because these Communist parties signally failed to reform themselves. Even where the leadership itself had become Eurocommunist, like the Spanish party or the British party, Carillo or McLennan were incapable of giving up power and following through the implications of democratisation in their own organisation. With the French party, the leadership was prepared to destroy a whole party to maintain its control. On the other hand, the Italian party became so open to everybody and so pluralistic that no-one knew what it stood for anymore. I didn't fully understand the mechanisms by which machine politics in the communist movement were maintained.

One of the things that really made me angry was the way at CP Congresses, instead of the executive committee leading the debate, so that splits on the executive would come out, it took this blanket view that they all shared the same views. So they stifled debate in the party because the platform was always supposed to agree. Everyone knew they were divided. That was part of the Stalinist tradition, that the leadership took a monolithic position. It really came from Lenin, that the party arrives at some truth and how it was supposed to get there became almost magical. It doesn't fall from heaven, it doesn't emerge from a static leadership, no-one has a monopoly of truth. For instance, this idea of the vanguard is an absurd idea, the party is not always going to be in the vanguard, it isn't always going to know, it is going to get it wrong.

We divided people into tankies (pro-Soviet) and then there was this new group in the party who I called economistic rather than Stalinist. They had a Stalinist practice in the labour movement, which was the belief that the trade unions were some kind of transmission belt: you win the leadership then sew up the organisation. You heard these horrible terms like 'sewing it up', and this whole language and behaviour which I despised. They disliked having open political debate and they didn't really believe in the capacity of ordinary people to make up their own minds.

It is wrong to see the relationship between members of the British CP and the Soviet Union as one of puppets and puppeteer. Certainly in the post-war period it was more complicated than that. You had a generation of leaders who were trained in Moscow and you had those party leaders who had grown up and imbibed a certain style of party organisation, practice and literature, which meant they operated in a Stalinist manner. They controlled from above the outcome in advance.

That began to break down during the period in which I became politically active because our generation were involved culturally in a world that wasn't anything to do with the CP or the Soviet Union but to do with the other events of May 1968. We were affected by a cultural change so that our socialism was linked to personal liberation, a loosening up of mores, having fun, sexual liberation and getting rid of those post-war restraints in the sense of the family controlling things. There was a sort of sea change going on; for me wearing jeans and having a dress code which enabled me to be a tomboy was really important because it meant you could ride bikes in the street, run, jump around, and it was OK. For a long time I had short hair and wore jeans. My mother complained, but it was a kind of statement about not being a frilly girl and not being moulded into a certain kind of femininity.

MOSCOW GOLD

When Reuben Falber was exposed as receiving Moscow gold, Martin Jacques wrote that he felt terrible about it, but I didn't react like that. I had never trusted the man - there were always apparatchiks in the party. I was a bit surprised about the Moscow gold because I thought, 'What a waste of money', but I wasn't shocked - even though all the time we were arguing for democratisation in the Soviet Union and against their interference, he was filtering money through.

There were people collecting money from the trade union movement who weren't aware of what was happening, not knowing the party was being subsidised. I thought it was despicable, but I always knew what I didn't like in the party and had always been opposed to the way the leadership operated. It wasn't just the old leadership. When my grouping, the Eurocommunists, won the leadership, I didn't like the way they behaved. But if you believe injustice is rooted in class oppression allied to oppression of women and of ethnic minorities then there is a case for an organisation which attempts to combine struggle around those and links them. I don't believe you can transform the relationship between men and women or the devastation of the environment without transforming the system of material production and in that sense I am still committed as a Marxist, although Marxism hasn't got all the answers and has to be allied to other kinds of theory and practice.

If you believe that there is a real difficulty, where do you go? What do you do? I believed in the Eurocommunist strategy. I once said I was a democrat and that is why I was a Communist. That is why I could never justify using people as means to some greater end, because if you do that then why should anyone be in favour of socialism?

It was a Stalinist ploy to present the split in the CP as having a class basis. A number of the Stalinists were very middle-class people, from Tony Chater to Palme Dutt. The economistic group were used to being in charge of the labour movement and there were a large lump of CP trade union officials who had this Stalinist notion of practice and politics and they were very opposed to Eurocommunism and said we were all middle-class.

It is true the party lost its working-class base, but it is not true that all the working-class base was Stalinist and the Eurocommunists were all middle-class. A number of the Eurocommunists came from a working-class background and we were part of the social advances of the 1960s and had gone to university. There were also some trade unionists who were Eurocommunist. It is not as simple as they would like to paint it.

It is also ludicrous to say that things like concern for the environment or for women's oppression are not issues of central concern for working-class people. If you argue that then you are either defining the working-class as male, which a lot of the Stalinists and the *Morning Star* people did, or you are saying that the only thing of importance is what people get in their wage packets - forget that they can't breathe the air or that their kids have got asthma. It is very difficult to sustain such a narrow view of what should be the concern of working-class politics today.

A SENSE OF LOSS

My CP background helped me to speak publicly and it gave me a sense of politics linked to debate and argument. One of the reasons I became inactive and left was that it didn't make me a mass leader or even a very good activist. I was too much absorbed in the party to be an effective activist. My brother is totally different. He became an excellent mass activist and leader; but partly it is just to do with energy, and partly it may be temperament. I found it took too much out of me and I wasn't very effective in those ways. It helped me as a speaker and helped me analyse and those things probably helped my career.

I have talked about this with my brother. Both in our different ways - me in university and he in local government - have been able to understand political machinations which other people are not aware are going on. We can both read them and not feel powerless about it. With my brother, people turn to him for advice about what is going on and for policy; he has a real grasp of that and I think that is something the CP had.

I also was part of a social network which I feel I have lost with the demise of the CP. My personal friendship network is something different, which I had before and after and still have, but there was a social network and contact there which was mutually self-reinforcing and I feel the lack of it. There was a continuity because you worked together and stood on those cold, wet mornings selling the *Morning Star* together or tramping around estates knocking on doors leafletting together or canvassing, so you had a lot of joint experiences and highs and lows.

That kind of shared commitment wasn't quite the same as a family, but when it collapsed I felt aware of being forced to be an atomised individual citizen where I can have my moral outrage and read the paper or write a letter but I don't feel part of a collective in the way that I did, and I haven't found anything to replace it with. I thought I had to be serious about the Labour Party because that is the only party of the left that's there but I find its culture so alien; it is so bureaucratic and so electorally oriented. The positive things that attracted people to the CP are not there in the Labour Party.

What I found oppressive about my family was the male dominance in it, and the strict division of labour between my parents. Their treatment of me was different from their treatment of my brother at times. My mother was a funny mixture because she always worked so she could have her own money and she always had a separate bank account. She never worked full-time; she worked part-time and said she did it so she could give us extra things. It was a funny kind of independence: when my father retired she worked to pay off the mortgage. On the other hand my father never cooked, very rarely washed up, she did all the cleaning while he did the garden - my mother did the front garden while he did the back garden - and my dad always did the car and DIY.

SQUARING THE CIRCLE

PAT DEVINE / NINA TEMPLE

PAT DEVINE is Senior Lecturer in Economics at the University of Manchester. He was born in 1937; his mother was an american communist and his father was a founding member of the British CP. Brought up in Manchester and evacuated during the war, his family later moved to London. He joined the YCL and did his national service in the RAF. After first opposing then supporting the party leadership over Hungary, he decided that the Eastern bloc countries were not socialist, and he pressed for internal change in the CP.

'Vote for me dad'

My mother and father met in the United States in Pittsburgh. My mother is American and her father was in the American Communist Party. They came from a Serbo-Croat immigrant background and they grew up in that community. She was active in the YCL in Pittsburgh and my father, who was from Motherwell in Scotland, was a foundation member of the British CP in 1920.

He had been sent by the British party to America to help the young American party, which consisted of mainly non-English-speaking people, to get themselves going. It was in the course of his touring round America and working with the unemployed in Pittsburgh that my father and mother met. They subsequently got married and then came back to Britain. I think my mother was 18 at the time and my father was 30.

They were communists when they met and remained so until the end, although my mother is still alive. I was born in 1937 and grew up with that background; I have a sister who was born in 1945. My mother had worked for the Comintern during the

1930s as a courier, taking money and documents in and out of Nazi Germany and China; and my father was for a period working in Moscow as a political representative at the Comintern. They came back in the mid-1930s. My father was the East London organiser of the party at the time of Cable street and my mother worked at King street, the CP headquarters. She was called Frieda Devine, but after she and my father split up she and Charlie Brewster got married, so Charlie was my stepfather.

I suppose my first political recollections were when we were living in Manchester. During the war my father was Lancashire and Cheshire district secretary and stood as party candidate in the 1945 general election and again in 1950. I remember quite vividly taking part in his electioneering activities when I was eight. Some comrades who lived in Preston, had one of these little square Minis which opened up, so that was the loudspeaker van with this huge horn tied on the top. I would go round with that and say, 'Vote for me dad!' over the loudspeaker and hand out leaflets. Ever since I can remember I lived in a communist household.

The party was huge at the time; in Manchester we were one of the places where the party pushed for what were called Joint Production Committees to be set up. These were committees of workers and management in order to discuss how to enhance the war effort. Because of the party's influence it was often able to play an instrumental role in getting these committees set up and the CP was seen as a respectable organisation.

During the war my father worked full-time for the party but so did my mother. I was, for several of the war years, evacuated to a boarding school, which was one of those progressive boarding schools that were quite common at the time. It was run by Beatrix Tudor-Hart and was called Fortis Green because it was evacuated from Fortis Green Road in North London. Quite a lot of party members as well as others on the left sent their children to this school, in Aspley Guise near Milton Keynes. There I met lots of people from a comparable background. For about the last year of the war I was living at home and they had, effectively, a housekeeper who looked after me when they weren't there. I have nothing but happy recollections of my time at this school, although my mother says she found it fairly traumatic when she came to visit me and I would always be very upset when she left.

I grew up on stories like the one my mother told about when she was a child; her mother spoke to her and said, 'Frieda something wonderful has happened in Russia, the workers have taken power, people like us'. Clearly there was this tremendous commitment to socialism and optimism that sooner or later it would happen in the west, but who knew when? My father was a staunch and loyal supporter of the Soviet Union, but then everyone in the party at this period was. They were not rank and file members of the party, they were active full-time workers.

It was not just that you felt different from your peers but you *were* different. My parents were both from working-class backgrounds but the party placed a great store on education and thought education was important, so the house had plenty of books in it and I was encouraged all the time to do well at school. I was greatly helped in this by Robin Jardine who was a lifelong lodger with my mother. He was from an educated Scottish background, also in the party, and was for many years the librarian at the *Daily Worker*, later *Morning Star*.

Of the gang of kids that I played around with in the street and in primary school I was the only one who went on to grammar school. You clearly were different, in the broad cultural sense which came from the perspective of being a Communist and having an international outlook, and you had a tremendous advantage. In the other more negative sense this idea of people in a special mould was also there, you did think you knew the answers.

I cannot say I recall this on a day to day basis, but there must have been an edge of not really being willing to listen or to hear what other people were saying. You knew a lot more and read the *Daily Worker* and pamphlets and you had an analysis. I found myself having this experience time after time over the years - that you were always asked for your point of view. People just sort of assumed because of your interest and background you would have an angle on it.

A SOCIALIST AT 14

I was brought up basically by my mother, not by my father, because of the absent father thing. He was out at meetings all the time. Then, during the war, my mother was also very active. She says she sometimes worries that she neglected my sister as a result of this but she never says it about me. I never felt neglected and my sister says neither did she. My father was a product of a Scottish, working-class traditional family, and was such a person himself. He expected the man's role to be like that, communist or not; and so if he had any spare time he didn't make the meal or clean the house, he would read the papers or go out to the pub or whatever.

We had very open discussion in the family, and one of the things I noticed at the time, and my children subsequently commented on, is how much more debate there was in our home compared to other children's.

My mother used to joke about a comrade in the branch in Ilford where we lived who would not allow anything in the house other than the *Daily Worker* because all the rest of it was 'capitalist lies'. That was regarded by her as being absurd: of course you should look at other views, otherwise how could you see what was wrong with them? I think there was, however, an assumption that there was something wrong with them.

My parents clearly did stand out in the community as different: they put a communist poster in the window for the local elections; both my parents stood as CP candidates in London in the 1950s. So all the neighbours would be aware of this and people I went to school with would be aware of this.

Although we knew our neighbours, we weren't really close to them because our community was much broader, it was the branch and the international scene. So we were clearly different in terms of the way we perceived ourselves in society and the way other people perceived us. I joined the YCL when I was 14, in 1951. I was keen to join as soon as I could because I was totally committed to communism. I had absorbed my parents' values and ideas and those of their friends and comrades; so it wasn't surprising, you absorb those ideas and they become your own.

I was a committed socialist and an atheist as early as I can remember. For about four years I was active in the YCL but not part of the leading group. I was at school and having a good time with my mates but I went along to weekly meetings and got a tremendous addition to my education. The YCL in those days was an educational organisation so we had speakers in. I remember one comrade coming along to the branch and giving an illustrated musical talk on *Die Fledermaus*, which was wonderful.

Until I went to grammar school I don't remember communism being an issue with my friends. I did encounter some problems at school from a couple of teachers and on a number of occasions I was discriminated against. For example, the English teacher would accuse me of submitting work that wasn't my own and used to give me marks that exceeded the maximum, like 13 out of 10, to indicate it couldn't possibly have been my own work. I knew he had a deep anti-communist view and therefore didn't like me. My sister Marge found this public exposure as a communist embarrassing, whereas I thrived on it; she would tend to keep it quiet while I would tell people if they didn't know already.

Marge was very anxious at one stage that Mum shouldn't stand as a candidate in the local elections because then it would be all over the papers again, but it wasn't a problem for me. I would go with my father to the local pitch where he used to hold open-air meetings, and as I got older I would sometimes get up and take a turn at making a speech. Much later, after I finished at university and came back, we used to regularly go to the party's pitch on the Southend front and take it in turns to get hecklers around. Once or twice he even persuaded me to go along with him when he had a pitch on Thursday lunchtime at Lincolns Inn Fields where all the city workers came out. It was quite good when my father and I started to do things together because it meant we were seeing a bit more of each other and we were a bit more in touch.

I recall in 1953, when Stalin died, I was 16. I was up one morning before my parents and I heard this news so I went up and woke them up and said, 'Stalin's died, what are we going to do?' as if somehow that was it.

The CP background stayed with me in the forces. I was in the RAF doing my national service, and because I had finished at school and had got a place to go to Oxford, was automatically put forward for a commission for officer training. So I was sent on various courses and usually did OK. But, once they had narrowed it down to a relatively small group, they then started doing security checks and at each of those stages in the process I was suddenly told, 'Sorry that's it'. This then stayed on my file so, whenever I arrived at a new posting and went to see someone, I ended up meeting the camp education officer for an interview who would start reading my papers and ask, 'Why didn't you apply for a commission?' I'd say, 'Just read on a bit ...' There was no question but that it was discrimination.

People who were from YCL or CP backgrounds were never allowed to do anything thought to be militarily sensitive, so you tended to end up being posted to, say, medical units. You rapidly learnt that the first thing you did when you arrived at your new posting was to look around for the other comrades, because there were bound to be quite a number of them there. They were also doing their National Service and there weren't all that many of these non-sensitive bases that they could be sent to. I remember at RAF Hospital Ely we started a *Daily Worker* round after we'd argued with the officer in charge who said we weren't allowed to do it.

DIVIDED LOYALTIES

When we were kids and lived in London we used to go on holiday together and might go out to Epping Forest on Sundays. We used to go to Blackpool for our holiday when we were in Manchester. We sometimes went to these places that seemed to be made available to the party, houses in the country. I never went to Eastern Europe with my parents, although they did go. My mother and Charlie Brewster later on went to the Soviet Union and the GDR.

In the case of my mother, the commitment was above all to the ideas and the objectives and values that she believed the party and the Soviet Union stood for. I don't really know about my father but I would say he was unshakably loyal to both the Soviet Union and the party. It was probably just as well, in one sense, that he died when he did in the early 1970s, because when those two loyalties started going in opposite directions, beginning in 1968, I think his heart was with the Soviet Union but his discipline meant at that stage he remained loyal to the CP.

Over Hungary my father supported the party line but my mother - and they had split up by then - did not. She and Charlie Brewster and I, in 1956, all opposed the Soviet intervention. In the local branch there was a large group opposed to it and many later left. I think, having been gravely shaken by the Twentieth Congress, they had started to talk things through and came to the conclusion that you couldn't just suppress a popular uprising if you believed in the principles of communism and workers' power. We argued that it had been a mistake to intervene. I was secretary of the YCL in Ilford and was quite openly arguing for that line, and there was some concern in the higher echelons of the borough about this.

The idea that you didn't have views of your own was not my experience. Democratic centralism does not mean you don't have your own views nor that you don't express them within the organisation; it means that whatever is finally decided you support. The various commissions that were set up to look at inner party democracy could be seen as looking at the way democratic centralism was supposed to operate and had not been operating.

Perhaps about 18 months after the Hungarian uprising, having been fighting against the leadership, I gradually found myself becoming convinced there was a lot in what they had been saying; so I changed my view on this and decided I had been wrong and it had been a necessary thing to happen after all. There was more evidence and a re-assessment of the factors - in the end what convinced me was the significance of the open border.

My position has evolved since then. When we came to 1968 and Czechoslovakia I fiercely opposed that, and continue to do so. At that time I contrasted the position with Hungary in 1956 - Hungarian border open, Czech border closed - and argued that the events in Czechoslovakia were orchestrated internally by the Czech party whereas the Hungarian party was being thrown overboard. In the late 1970s, early 1980s, I came to the conclusion that these countries were not socialist after all, and therefore you could not justify an intervention on the grounds that it was safeguarding socialism. It was just to do with the control of the country by the regime, and the fact that the Soviet Union did not want within its sphere of influence a government that was hostile.

I don't take that Trotskyist view which argues that these countries were state capitalist. I believe that they were a new social formation that Marx hadn't envisaged, perhaps building on or developing out of his concept of the Asiatic mode of production. What was evolving during this period was my view, which had become very explicit by the mid-1960s, that socialism had to be democratic. Elements of what we used to call bourgeois democracy were not just a mask; they were necessary conditions for a fully functioning democracy. So you had to have the right for there to be more than one party, right to free speech, freedom of information, and these were central to socialism. A group of us were arguing that, just as you can have democratic and undemocratic capitalism, so you can have different forms of socialism. Eventually we came to the conclusion that you can't have socialism without democracy, it is a contradiction in terms.

My father and I didn't agree. He remained a Stalinist all his life and didn't change his views. We discussed it. I wouldn't say we would fall out about it. You didn't fall out personally, you just disagreed. But my mother's views evolved in much the same way as mine did, and she changed her views even more radically than I did because of where she started from.

The party gradually became out of touch, not in terms of individuals being out of touch with other individuals, but as an institution which became increasingly irrelevant to society. I have been more or less working to change the party for the whole of my adult life and I suppose I stayed in it for three reasons.

First, I believed in the values of communism and still do; second, because it seemed to me to be important to belong to something rather than deciding to act just on your own. Lastly, I thought that, particularly from the 1970s onwards, the party could be changed in ways I and people I was associated with thought was essential. We felt if it were to change in those directions then this sense of growing irrelevance could be reversed. I suppose it was not until right towards the end, in the late 1980s, that I began to realise that actually the party wasn't going to be changed, and so from about 1986-7 I ceased to be as actively involved as I had been.

THE PARTY IS OVER

We wanted to stop this dependence on the Soviet Union that still lingered on. In 1978-9, I remember, Dave Cook and I were on the party's second inner party democracy commission and we were part of the opposition which produced a minority report for the 1979 Congress called 'Alternative Proposals'. One of the things we were talking about was the Soviet and East European connection. We put forward a proposal that this should be severed, in the sense that there should be no holidays accepted from these countries because this placed you in a situation of dependence, however subtle. Just for the sake of it we added 'and also we think this practice of CP political committee members receiving bottles of spirits from Soviet and East European embassies at Christmas should be discontinued.' Reuben Falber, who was the chair of this commission, just went absolutely apoplectic. He thought we were so small-minded and mean-spirited to take this view, but we thought it was essential to establish the independence of the British party in these subtle cultural ways.

I am not one of those who feel that the decision to end the party at its last Congress was wrong, because I had thought for some time that the party as an institution was finished, and culturally unable to adapt to change. What I had hoped for was that it would change in directions which were still committed to a socialist transformation of society. My view at the end was that it should announce that it was disbanding in two years and use those two years to enter into discussions with other socialist groupings but particularly with elements from the green movement, to form some new eco-socialist red-green coalition. What in fact happened was that it went in the opposite direction and formed Democratic Left - where is it now and what does it stand for?

The history and the lessons that were painfully learnt are in danger of being lost because there is no continuity. I suppose I am talking about left Eurocommunist notions of hegemony, historic blocs, the importance of ideas, consent rather than coercion. If you are less interested in political strategy than day to day reaction then these notions are bound to seem abstract, but they are still important. They are premised on a democratic society, but they have a lot to tell us about how democracy can be deepened and how political organisations can and can't act if they are to try and help this process along. There is an awful lot there for the next generation to take up, in the struggle for transforming society and looking beyond capitalism. I am now involved in the Green Study Group, and attempts to form a Green Left.

PERSONAL POLITICS

I think the 1960s period was tremendously important, although I don't think the sex, drugs and rock and roll thing impinged directly. What most of all had a huge impact on me was the emergence of the feminist movement towards the end of the 1960s and then into the 1970s. This, I think, was probably the single biggest influence that I would be conscious of as having really caused me to work on myself to change in important ways.

Ann Long and I were still married at the time, with three children; we grew up believing in equality between men and women, and we always practised that as we saw it. But our view of what that meant was radically transformed as a result of this period and led to important changes in our personal household relationships.

What I got from the values of the party was the need to realise your ability to the full. For me what was very valuable, and has remained so, is that the measure of success was very different from conventional success. In my world, success would really be to lead a life which combined a contribution to making the world a better place, in whatever way, with decent relationships with other people and also, if you were lucky, to be happy and enjoy yourself. The fact that someone makes a lot of money or becomes famous was regarded as being largely irrelevant. Conventional definitions of success and status were not things I was brought up to attach any importance to, and I think that has lasted.

Most people I know from my times in the party are either from the public sector/professional spheres on the one hand, or they are in working-class jobs on the other. But what they are not are business people or accountants.

I think Ann and I did quite consciously think about what was the best way to bring the kids up, what sorts of experiences it would be good for them to be introduced to. We consciously were keen to expose them to a set of values, so there was constant discussion and talk. These were values of socialism, anti-capitalism, the worth and potentiality in people; and I suppose all three children, in their different ways, have got - in some senses - a lot of these values but reworked and reshaped according to their times. They are all teachers of one sort or another.

NINA TEMPLE was born in 1956, the same year her parents joined the CP. Her mother was a school head and her father worked for the Central Bureau for Educational Visits and Exchanges, until he was forced out because of his politics and became director of Progressive Tours. She was brought up on a council estate in Westminster and went to school in Camden. After taking a degree in engineering she worked full-time for both the YCL and the CP during the split of the 1980s. She took over as general secretary of the CP in 1990 and now heads the Democratic Left.

LIFE AFTER STALIN

My mother Barbara was born in the East End and brought up in Plaistow. Her parents were both Scottish and her father was a mason. They had moved down to get work in the docks in the 1920s, he was a shipwright and a skilled craftsman.

My father Landon's parents lived in Bridgewater and his father was a silent movie orchestra conductor - when the talkies came in he was unemployed.

My father won a scholarship to Oxford, which was a complete change of lifestyle from his poor background. My mother went to the Slade School of Art. She got evacuated to Oxford during the war when she was about 18, so they met in Oxford.

Landon was in the Labour Club in Oxford at the same time as Denis Healey, who was in the Communist branch there. He got a first in two years because everything was squashed up against the war. They got married and lived quite a Bohemian lifestyle. They went to Cornwall for a while, she was painting and he was beating copper pots, so the Communist Party hadn't loomed into their life at that point.

After the war, Landon did Voluntary Service Overseas for a bit and Barbara became a teacher; later he worked for the Central Bureau for Educational Visits and Exchanges. They had four children, but one of my brothers died in his early twenties.

My parents didn't join the CP until 1956, the year I was born. They weren't involved in the party until quite late on in life. They joined after Stalin had been denounced, because they thought that would mean communism with a human face would come about. They had always been on the left. They had also got involved with various campaigns and by the time I was a kid my father was very involved in tenants' associations, so it would have been natural for them to join the CP. As I grew up they were ordinary party members, helping at *Daily Worker* bazaars, and my father got very active with meetings.

My mother had a large family and didn't have time to go to meetings, and the party branch didn't handle that well at all. They thought she was an unimportant comrade because she didn't attend branch meetings. She was working in primary schools; she eventually became headmistress of an infants school in East London, she felt she was doing quite a lot to help disadvantaged kids, and that it was important, but other comrades didn't think it was.

The last straw for her was when someone came round with her party card signed up and gave it to my dad - so she left the CP in the 1970s. Even though by then I had joined the YCL, I agreed with her and thought she was right to leave because she was being treated badly. You wouldn't call my mother a radical feminist; but it was a matter of respect, that the party wasn't respecting her as a human being and the fact that she looked after the kids when Landon was out doing things. He was very active by then and a local CP candidate, he was also secretary of the Joint Federation of Westminster Tenants Associations.

We were living in the heart of London, in St John's Wood, on a council estate. It was a weird background in a sense because there was so much wealth around and yet we were in a council estate which had been built at the end of the war in a wave of optimism that the workers could live anywhere. When the block was first built it was called Starling House - it is in an estate called the Birdcage locally, which is made up of blocks with different birds' names. Starling House was apparently dubbed Stalin House because Russia was very popular at that time, being an ally in war.

'NINA, GO BACK TO RUSSIA'

My father spent a lot of time out at meetings. My main memories of him as a child are either on holidays or in politics: that was the way to see daddy, selling the *Daily Worker*. But he did take long holidays of five or six weeks and we would all go off as a family. We didn't really have any money so we would go off in old bangers to the continent. We had marvellous holidays as kids.

I can remember as a young child going door to door on *Daily Worker* sales, and I used to quite like it because people saved up all their chocolate bars and it was like a chocolate collection really! Landon stood for election in the late 1950s/early 1960s which did cause me problems because there were a lot of Cold War attitudes around still, so I used to get lots of, 'Nina, go back to Russia'. You would think my parents were Russian mad to give me the name Nina; in fact I got it because my mum saw the film *Ninotchka* when she was pregnant with me and she called me after that. I used to get a lot of taunting as a child from kids on the estate because we had posters and leaflets about my dad around, and it was an extraordinary thing to be a Communist. I think it was to do with politics that they never left there. They had opportunities when they could have moved away.

The biggest political excitment I can remember as a child was the campaign to get housing rather than hotels in Marylebone, which was successful. The council had agreed planning permission for hotels, and the party started a campaign that it should be housing at low rents so that working-class people could live in central London. It was creative. They picketed the council and the Dorchester Hotel, so it was quite exhilarating to be involved.

My father was always so busy my mother was left looking after us a lot of the time. He was working at the Central Bureau for Educational Visits and Exchanges. He would come home before a meeting, rush in and madly type and duplicate, then rush out again.

It affected my family badly when the boss at the Central Bureau left. Landon applied for his job, but because he was in the Communist Party they weren't going to let him get the promotion he had earned. All sorts of dirty tricks happened, including allegations made against him. A guy in the organisation who was gay was made by MI5 to denounce Landon. Eventually this man arranged a meeting with Landon to tell him he hadn't wanted to do it but they had threatened to expose him. There were still Cold War attitudes at that point and that cast a shadow over the family. Landon was driven out of the job altogether in a very unpleasant way. The *Sunday Times* were prepared to do an exposé on the case but the party decided against it because it would have created a bad image for the party, and might put people off joining. He was so loyal he didn't pursue it, which was frustrating and led to embitterment but not disenchantment.

After that he ended up taking over Progressive Tours, which was a nightmare really; it was bankrupt at that time, in the early 1970s, but the party couldn't afford to close it down. It would have bankrupted the party. So they asked Landon to take it over. I remember my mother was very upset because one of the CP hierarchy said to Landon that he would have to take it over because, after the Central Bureau thing, he was a broken man and nobody would employ him. She felt very angry. She wanted him to do something he wanted to do, like becoming an architect, while he felt he had to have a job in order to keep a family with four children. It meant he dropped out of party activity altogether working all hours instead at Progressive Tours and turning the great millstone slowly round.

He had a lot to do with Russia then, and came across its bureaucracy, and developed quite a torn relationship with it. He was more loyal than he had ever been, so when Afghanistan happened he was ambiguous - having earlier condemned the invasion of Czechoslovakia. At the same time he was face to face with the actual frustrations of a ridiculous system where nobody would take any decisions or show initiative or arrange anything effectively in any way. He didn't have time for holidays and used to come home every evening exhausted and uptight. The party was completely unappreciative. Landon found out much later on that Reuben Falber would write cheques to the CP from Progressive Tours without Landon knowing about it.

The travel agency would reach protocols with the Soviet Union which were favourable, but they were less favourable than the ones reached with Thomson Holidays. The Soviet Union had a funny relationship with the West. They would give Landon a favourable deal because it was the party, but they would also see a big capitalist company and believed that this would bring thousands of people in so they would give a much more favourable deal to them, although Landon was, in fact, sending more people than Thomson. He tried to become specialist and establish a niche, for instance by sending the English National Opera across to the Kirov Ballet, and opening up cultural exchanges.

SCHOOL POLITICS

There was that sense of being different. We went on demonstrations against the Vietnam War, like Grosvenor Square, and I was wheeled on the first Aldermaston CND march. It affected the children very differently. I was number three so it wasn't so awkward for me, and in some ways I found it a great advantage because now I can feel at home with people from all backgrounds.

I went to school just as grammar schools were changing to comprehensives. I went to Camden School for girls, which was founded by the suffragettes, so it was a nice atmosphere, and a good antidote to the Communist Party in that it was very committed to the liberal tradition, so I learnt a lot about human rights and free speech. Before that I had gone to the junior school next to the estate.

At school I stood as a Communist candidate in school elections and usually came second to Labour. I was naturally argumentative. We did things like going on Vietnam demos together as a class, and I brought the whole school out on strike over getting rid of school uniforms. We set up a school council, which I was the secretary of, with a representative from each year, and teachers and heads and I gave reports to the school assembly.

My party background wasn't really a problem - although my history teacher tried to get me not to do history O level because she said I was useless at it. She said that the lesson of the 1926 General Strike was that general strikes in a democracy were unconstitutional and we had a debate about it.

In religion I can remember my RE teacher being in tears because I said I had no religion at all: I could respect her belief in God but for me it was no more relevant than saying I believe there is a giant carrot in the sky, and she was in tears over that.

The party background did affect me in the sense that my

parents didn't have time to do the normal things with me, like swimming club and ballet, and I had a row with them about the Brownies, which they didn't want me to join because of the King and Queen thing. So I joined the Woodcraft Folk, the co-operative society youth movement, in the end but I got expelled from that! The organiser didn't turn up one night and the older ones tried to buy booze but nobody could buy any, so they decided I looked young enough to buy some for my mum. So I did and was expelled without any proper procedures. Eventually they wrote to me saying I could rejoin but I told them where to go.

COMMUNISTS OR CALVINISTS?

My mother was very tolerant and we spent most of our time with her; she was a strong influence on all of us. My father did take us for big walks in the country maybe once a month.

We were brought up heading into the 1960s, which was a big clash with the Communist view of what is right and wrong. My biggest brother was the first to rebel. I can remember when he grew his hair right down and my father went barmy and my mother said, 'Don't be ridiculous'. He was really into the Kinks, so there were big battles over pop music and hair length. I can remember my mother bought me and my sister psychedelic trousers for Christmas once and were really delighted but Landon was furious about it. There was a kind of Calvinism in the communist tradition, a prudity, which affected him deeply.

Another battleground was our education: he was determined we would be 'useful' to society which seemed to mean 'not creative'. This was very disparaging to my mother with her fine arts degree, but in fact also disparaging to him since he had studied history. He felt we all needed to be scientists and help make society a better place; it was a very reductive view of what is and isn't valid.

Julian wanted to study history but Landon insisted he did architecture, which he thought was useful. So Julian went to Cambridge to study architecture but after one year he had had enough so he changed to history, then did film after that and went his own way. Stephen, my middle brother, was really gifted in science so he was happy studying physics at Oxford when he died. At school I would probably have drifted towards languages but under Landon's pressure I did maths and chemistry A level.

I had decided that when I finished I would take a year off school and travel abroad, but Landon was convinced that if I did I would get pregnant and waste my life. So he got a person at Imperial College, who I think he got to know of through a party comrade, to come and see me. He was a very nice man and I was quite taken by the electromicroscope - you could look through it and see individual atoms - so I agreed to do an engineering degree. I quite enjoyed it but eventually realised it wasn't me. I had decided to leave when my brother died suddenly; my course seemed a minor issue in the overwhelming family grief, so I stayed and finished it.

I had joined the YCL in my neighbourhood; it had about 35 members including some nice young men and it was very much a social activity. I became the Westminster YCL social organiser and started running a disco on the estate above the laundry which was quite successful, with about 200 people coming along.

It was all going swimmingly - this was the late 1960s - but disaster struck when the branch was taken over by Stalinists. All these much older people came in - there were a lot of young working-class men working in Selfridges' warehouse - and the new group got rid of the branch secretary by saying he was a poofter. The whole thing changed completely. I was at a YCL disco on the estate with a lot of my friends and suddenly the music went off and Fergus Nicholson gave a speech about why Russia was right to invade Czechoslovakia. I was mortified and embarrassed, so that was the end of the YCL disco. The YCL was split from 1968 so I was very partisan on the side of the anti-Stalinists. What I don't really understand is why I stayed in it after that.

A BRUTAL MACHINE

Part of the YCL was very committed to youth culture and part of it saw the YCL as a youth wing of the CP. The CP culture was an inhibitor in really getting stuck in to the youth movement of the 1960s. If I hadn't had a CP background I probably would have taken some drugs. As far as the sex thing is concerned the

CP didn't stop me at all, I was very much a girl of my time.

I started my first full-time job with the London YCL, although my parents were very against me doing that and we had a big family row over it. Landon was a loyal party member and active in tenants' associations, but I think he knew the party machine was a brutal place and didn't want me to be smashed up by it.

My parents were very critical of the Soviet Union. When the book *Let History Judge* by Medvedev came out, with accounts of what Stalin had done in some detail, quite a lot of Communists were trying to say it was a pack of lies but my parents both believed what was in the book. But Landon remained very loyal to the party - later on when I was trying to change the CP into what it is now, I can remember my father coming to see me and referring to the Democratic Left constitution, which I had helped draft, as 'crap', saying there was nothing in it and we were throwing everything away.

I was very affected by Vietnam and it gave me the feeling that solidarity could achieve things. When I was selling *Challenge* in Church street market I met some Italians. They stayed in my house for two weeks and I went to Milan when I was 17. I stayed there for about six weeks, working on *Festa de L'Unita*, preparing for the week-long festival of the Italian CP newspaper, which was a big experience for me because I got to know a lot about the Italian CP.

I was on demonstrations with a million people against fascism, and after a festival I went off with some people whose parents and grandparents had been in the partisans - we just walked all over the mountains and stayed in the stone huts they had stayed in during the war. I got to know what it was like to be of the left and for it to be really a mass thing in contrast to the party in Britain, which was always very isolated. I think if I hadn't had that experience I probably would not have become so devoted to politics here, because I knew from then on that the British CP would never make a breakthrough.

Two years later the YCL sent me back to Italy to join in events to mark the 30th anniversary of the ending of the war. I was 19 and it was extraordinary. I came across Soviet bureaucrats for the first time and saw them making these great speeches about socialism and the new world; and then in the evening three of them tried to break my door down and rape me. I was staying next to Santiago Carillo, the Spanish CP leader, and luckily he had four bodyguards who sorted it out.

So I saw really sharply the hypocrisy that was going on. The Russians tried to get me to speak on behalf of the youth of Europe at this rally, but I refused to do it and they were really pissed off. I didn't go abroad for the YCL for 15 years after that because I was so disgusted by it. There was also a gravy-train culture in the YCL where you got trips abroad, and I didn't want to have anything to do with it.

AN AWFUL CHOICE

In 1982 I finished working with the YCL and I didn't want to work for the party. I had applied for various jobs. But the bust-up between *Marxism Today* and the *Morning Star* burst out just then, and I was the only person on the political committee, apart from Martin Jacques, who was supporting *Marxism Today*. I was caught by that. There was a vacancy for the head of press and publicity for the CP and, if I hadn't agreed to do it, Gerry Cohen, whose views and practice I strongly disagreed with, would have got. So I had this awful choice of leaving Martin in the lurch with Gerry Cohen becoming more powerful, or staying and helping Martin out, which I thought would only take a year or two but it took a lot longer.

It wasn't the party that I put first in that instance but my own views. It was like a sucking-in process: you made a stand on one thing, they did something else, so it was like a game of chess. Later on I proposed that Ian McKay move over to London district, which left a vacancy for national organiser. And since he was going into the lion's den I felt morally bound to fill his place. I stopped to have my first baby in 1986 which would have been a good moment to leave. I was seriously thinking about it, but they tempted me back with a part-time arrangement doing journalism for *Seven Days* magazine. At that time I was looking at my own personal situation with the baby and this dream offer of really interesting, flexible, part-time work floated in but it proved to be fateful because I was still there years later.

At the end of the day I stayed because of all the time I had put into it; I had to choose between walking away from it, and seeing it fall apart or becoming part of a very sectarian rump, or trying to change it.

So, for me, the worst time was the end of the 1980s when the CP was imploding and I was right in the middle of it. It was a very uncreative period when I got to know hardly anyone outside the CP. It was very frustrating and in many ways I resent the way I used those years, although if I had missed them I would not have had the opportunity to do what I do now, which I really enjoy.

Since we have been Democratic Left I have got to know lots more people. One of the initiatives we set up was a committee on voting reform that I chair, with two Tory MPs on it and people from other parties; we want to push for the referendum on PR. There is also Unions '96 where we have built up relations with about 20 unions.

I feel much more comfortable working for Democratic Left than I did for the CP. When I took up the job of CP secretary in January 1990 I thought there was a 10 per cent chance of anything useful coming out of it and a 90 per cent chance of there being no point at all. It was a horrible moment of realisation that, however much we had fought Stalinism and tried to uphold democratic values, we were within the framework of the communist parties, with all that meant; and that the Communist Party could not be reformed - it had to go.

DECENT VALUES

I had this ridiculous media coverage when I took the job on - 'mother of two takes on job just as communism collapses in flames': I was doing 10 or 20 media interviews a day at the same time as thinking, why the hell have I done this?

During the transformation into Democratic Left I had to win the passive support of older Communists. I went around the country and spoke to most remaining members and put it to them they had a choice: the whole thing dying, or making a radical break that they might not like or agree with but would mean us taking forward something of the best of what they had done in the past. We still believed ordinary people could have some effect in changing the world, and I had to sit down and think about the real values of the CP and why I joined. The heart of it wasn't the ideology, slogans or dogma about overthrowing the state or dictatorship of the proletariat; most people joined out of a belief in social justice and solidarity and decent values. I asked what was most precious to them of their beliefs, which could live on in some form appropriate to our times.

When I took over the job I was the youngest person in the office by two decades, and it was the same at party meetings. So it was a strange experience. I got a terrible post for four or five months but at least we were having this discussion we should have had 20 or 30 years before. I got such spleen vented on me: people said they had wanted to die a Communist, I was dishonouring people who died in Spain. And I would say we were trying to take forward the best of that tradition.

I feel now that the Communist Party had basic values of solidarity and fighting for social justice, which had a long history in Britain but they were constrained into a Bolshevik mould for most of this century but now that mould is broken. One of the little rivulets that has flowed out of it is the Democratic Left. Even if there had been a reforming CP general secretary years ago they probably would not have been able to do much because the culture was so conservative. It took a lot of different things coming together - like George Matthews exposing Stalin's involvement in the 'British Road to Socialism' - to break the belief in the status quo, to destroy things so they could be re-invented in a different way.

I have had to shed a hell of a lot of what I grew up with. I learned how impotent the Communist Party was in its isolation and how powerful it was when it wasn't isolated. For instance, when we worked with tenants in my neighbourhood it did physically stop being a little party meeting in a front room and started reaching out to people, saying let us do things together to make things better.

Change can happen more easily than you might think if people are creative and network together; but it happens terribly slowly if you cut yourself off and have a rigid plan of what you think is going to happen, and that plan doesn't fit with the world, and you are too rigid to adjust. I no longer believe in a set of policies or a party which says it has got a way to show others, but I do believe groups of people can act as catalysts to stimulate people as long as they are prepared to learn. If that is a process they go with it can be creative and fruitful in bringing about change.

I believe in some basic values, the basic values of democratic socialism, with a strong emphasis on participation. The rift between the Second and Third Internationals was a mistake, and it was ridiculous for Communists to think they had a superiority. I think I was as much shaped by the liberal tradition as by the communist tradition and I believe in those ideals as passionately as I ever did.

The party wasted a huge amount of time. I have had to learn a lot about management. And for an organisation that thought it was going to change the world it took so little interest in how the world was changing. There was all this claptrap about scientific socialism and yet the whole process of work and management was changing rapidly but the Communist Party remained frozen as it had been organised for 70 years: it was in a time warp really.

In terms of my own career prospects, the six years I spent in the internicine warfare in the CP were not good, but now I feel what I am doing is something that will lead to other work I can do; and I am learning other things I can apply elsewhere. I feel I am bringing about more change now than if I were an MP. Being a backbench MP for the Labour Party between 1979 and now would have been very frustrating and, anyway, that doesn't really attract me. It might attract me if political institutions were to change and PR was won, but the present relationship between MPs and the people is not very meaningful.

I am beginning to think about what I do next, partly because I want the Democratic Left to survive after me. I am interested in campaigning and have ideas about how certain groups should campaign. I am interested in cultural transformation I suppose.

Now I am a parent myself I realise how hard it is and I am a little humbler in my criticisms of the efforts of my own parents. I am very committed to keeping real flows of communication open with my children; it is terribly important to be able to talk to them and talk through things, rather than them thinking you are going to give them such a mouthful that they best not tell you whatever it is.

That is my big ambition with my children: to be able to still talk to them about their personal problems as they are going through their teenage years. I hope that, in this respect, the experience of my family is very different from my childhood. But you'd have to talk to my children in thirty years time to check that.

VOYAGE ROUND MY FATHER

BRIAN POLLITT

BRIAN POLLITT was born in London in 1936, the son of CP general secretary Harry Pollitt and schoolteacher Marjorie Brewer. He attended school in London, leaving to work for a short time at Collets, the left-wing bookchain, before completing his national service in the Royal Artillery. He graduated from Cambridge University with first class honours in Economics and Politics and carried out post-graduate research on agrarian reform in Cuba from 1963-68. He has since pursued an academic career, working in universities in Cambridge, the USA, Chile, Australia and Nicaragua. Since 1975 he has lectured at the Institute of Latin American Studies at the University of Glasgow, and is currently editing the works of Maurice Dobb.

ARRESTED ON HONEYMOON

I was aware from a very early age that my father, Harry Pollitt, was an important and controversial figure. I knew he was the leader of the British Communist Party and, at the age of nine, was disappointed to learn that the Politburo was not, as I had supposed, his office. I knew him to be immensely proud of his Lancashire working-class background. He was born in 1890 and was one of six children. The material poverty of his family was reflected by the death in infancy of three of these children. He worshipped his mother whom he regarded as the most important personal and political influence on his early life. As a boy, he worked part-time with her in a textile mill before leaving school to become a boilermaker's apprentice at the Gorton Tank works in Manchester. He was active in politics from an early age. His mother's 21st birthday present to him, dated 22 November 1911, says much about their extraordinary relationship: it was Volume One of Marx's *Capital*.

My mother's background was very different. She was illegitimate and was fostered by an eccentric woman with no other children. She did not know her father and knew herself to have been unwanted by her real mother. She was an intelligent child and won a scholarship to Christ's Hospital, which was an elite girls' school in London. She later trained as a schoolteacher. She joined the CP before she met my father in 1923. They married in 1925. As a youth I was very impressed to learn that a fellow-guest at their modest honeymoon hotel turned out to be a member of the Special Branch who arrested my father shortly thereafter. He was charged with sedition and was jailed for 12 months. My mother was prominent in the campaign to release him and other CP leaders imprisoned at the same time. These activities were officially deemed to be conduct unbecoming a teacher, and she was punished by being barred for life from exercising her profession. From that time on she worked either as a secretary or receptionist.

I was aware that I had two very different kinds of parent. My mother was an educated middle-class professional of unconventional upbringing in the south of England. My father was a working-class Lancastrian, proud of his northern accent and roots.

Within the household, my mother had the job of answering political questions from the children. This was partly because my father was often away and partly because he felt he had quite enough of politics outside the home. My mother was a political activist as long as I recall. She was on the CP London District Committee for some years and was a parliamentary candidate for Hendon North after 1950. If anything she followed the twists and turns in the Party line more readily than my father. In 1939, for example, she did not share my father's heretical view on the nature of the war. However, since I was three years old at the time this meant nothing to me and I was generally unaware of any political differences between them.

DISRUPTIONS OF POLITICS AND WAR

My childhood was disrupted by both politics and World War II. In 1938 my mother won an English Speaking Union scholarship to go to the USA and was away for six months. I was two at the time and was sent to live with family friends, but don't now know which. In 1940, during the London blitz, my sister and I were both boarded in girls' schools in the home counties. And in 1944-45, with the rocket attacks on London, my sister was sent to live with relatives in Swindon and I went to Manchester. My recollections of early home life are thus confused. I certainly seem to have lacked a fixed abode, whether physical or emotional. Moreover, when my father and I were at home at the same time, our contact could be very limited since he often left for work before I got up and came home after I'd gone to bed. And of course my mother worked full-time which meant that during my primary school years the house was usually empty when I came home. This all encouraged me to be quite self-sufficient. I learned from an early age to let myself into the house and to make my own tea and I spent a lot of time (some of it very anti-socially) on the streets in a gang with my pals. From about the age of five I could be baby-sat at a distance, if necessary, being able to knock on the bedroom wall to the next door neighbour in case of need. More often I would be left in my sister, Jean's, charge. She was more than four years older than me and her frequent exercise of authority when I was young led to rather stormy times between us in later years.

My father was the Party's leading orator and the public meeting was a prime form of political activity so he was continually travelling up and down the country, spending many days away from London. He also represented the British Party on frequent trips abroad. I always felt his absence and very much looked forward to his return. I don't think any compensating closeness developed between me and my mother. She and I had spent many months apart since I was two years old and perhaps this affected things. In any event, I certainly didn't feel that my company was indispensable to her. This was well illustrated when I was 11 and, having passed the 11 plus exam, was about to go from primary school to grammar school. My mother had mobilised British families to send parcels and letters, and sometimes to provide holiday homes, for orphaned children of the French Resistance who lived in a home south of Paris. It seems that she was asked what the orphanage could do for her in exchange. The upshot was that I was sent there for the summer of 1947. I was judged (rightly) to be capable of travelling by myself on both train and boat, being met only in Paris; but I remember my weeks in the orphanage, where classes were uninterrupted throughout the summer, as being deeply lonely and unhappy. My mother told me it would be splendid experience for me and I would go to grammar school already speaking French (which I did). But a less charitable view would see all this as a rationalisation for having your child out of the way during the long summer holidays. Other holidays were more agreeable, being generally associated with gang life on the streets or with games in my house where all the other kids could come because my parents were never there during weekdays.

JEWISH ALLIES

There was obviously a price to be paid for being a child in the household of CP activists, especially if both parents worked and money was tight. But one of the easy things for CP children of my generation was that for a number of years outside hostility for our parents' politics was muted. During World War II - or at least from 1941 - the USSR was our ally, and Stalin led the heroic Red Army which, in Churchill's words, 'tore the guts out' of the common Nazi enemy. Cinema newsreels then spoke of 'our Soviet allies', and not, as later during the Cold War, of the 'Red menace'. I knew my father was a controversial figure but the people whose homes we visited, or who visited us in our home, obviously worshipped him. And, on more public occasions, I used to witness, as a boy, thousands of people applauding him in the great rallies in Trafalgar Square or in the big arenas of Earls Court or Haringey. So while there was some sense of isolation in my street, primary school or neighbourhood, where there were no other boys or friends who came from communist families, in those mass meetings I could see my father as a charismatic popular leader - which he was. Moreover, despite its domestic weakness, the CP was part of a powerful international movement led by our friends and allies, the Soviets. A lot of this was to change in later life, but up to the age of 11 and the onset in

1947-48 of the Cold War, I felt quite unthreatened by my father's political notoriety.

This began to change when I passed the 11-plus exam in 1947 and went to Preston Manor County Grammar School in Wembley, Middlesex. The school drew most of its pupils from the predominantly middle-class area in which it was located. I lived outside that and only two other kids from my primary school went there in my year. My grammar school years coincided with the onset of the Cold War and it became routine to encounter abuse of my father, often as an extension of abuse of me. The teachers generally observed a self-denying ordinance not to make public play of my background, but from time to time a comment in class on world affairs might be followed by, for example, 'Of course, Brian Pollitt might not agree'. But in the playground - and outside school as well - I became accustomed to hear my father called 'a Commie bastard' or worse, and I became 'a Red bastard' by extension. Such remarks were usually meant to provoke a fistfight but after a while these became tiresome and I developed some pacific lines of patter calculated to avoid them. I countered the jeer that my father was a bastard - widely thought to be a quite unavoidable challenge to physical combat - with the entirely accurate rejoinder that 'He isn't, actually - but it's true that my mother was born out of wedlock'. In time one of my teachers learned of this and a letter was written home to report that I was broadcasting my mother's illegitimacy.

This sort of problem reinforced my friendship with the three Jewish boys in my class. For them, playground conflicts could provoke anti-semitic epithets such as 'greedy Jew-boy' and this seemed to parallel some of my own difficulties. The relationship was reinforced at the age of 14 or 15 when I decided to end the charade of joining in the Lord's Prayer at morning assembly and stood there quietly with my eyes open instead. This prompted another letter from school to home, stating that I required parental permission for such conduct. My parents wrote back saying 'Our son has our permission to do what he thinks right in this matter'. Evidently fearing the spread of my subversion - which initially attracted one or two likeminded classmates - I was excused from attending assembly altogether and spent the time with the Jewish boys excused on religious grounds. But I liked singing carols and madrigals and retained my position in the school choir. In general, as with most of my Jewish friends, external prejudice and hostility seem to have reinforced, rather than weakened, the beliefs I inherited from my parents; and as I grew up my response to an increasingly pervasive anti-Communism was greater political activism. I joined, and was active, in my local YCL from 1951 and my subsequent entry into the CP was delayed only for the two years of my military service.

The social circle of party members in which my family moved was a broad one. At one end of the spectrum were quite wealthy families. The household of Olive Parsons - who died a short time ago at a very great age - was one such. As a boy I used to visit what seemed to me to be her enormous house in Hampstead, where I played for hours with the elaborate train sets outgrown by her sons. Another was the household of Barney Letsky and his family. Of Russian-Jewish origin, he was an industrial chemist, and while we travelled to his home in North London by trolley bus, he usually drove us back again by car. This was a rare treat. There was a quite different setup when my father stood as a parliamentary candidate for Rhondda East in 1945. Throughout the campaign, I stayed with Annie and Trevor Powell. Annie was a well-known Welsh communist and Trevor worked with the Cooperative Society. They lived at 12 Railway View, Llwynypia, one of a row of back-to-back terrace houses with the lavatory at the bottom of the blackened strip of ground that passed for a garden. I remember standing in the kitchen sink to have my knees scrubbed, and the way the bedroom window rattled at night as the trains went by. That house was very like the one in which my father was brought up in Droylesden, Lancashire and it reminded me of the homes of some of his relatives in Manchester in 1944 and after.

I associate those weeks in South Wales with scrambling over and around the hills and slag heaps of the Rhondda Valley, learning to tickle trout in the few unpolluted streams and attending innumerable pithead meetings addressed by my father. Waiting for the election result outside the Town Hall, it seemed inconceivable that he wouldn't win. In point of fact, he nearly did, polling over 15,000 votes and apparently winning a majority of the residential constituency vote. But he went down on the overseas votes posted home along traditional Labour lines by the soldiers. In the next general election, in 1950, his vote fell to 4000 so it was easy for me to chart the Party's decline from its high points to the lower ones. He was very much at home campaigning in South Wales. He always stayed in the homes of old party comrades - a practice he kept up all his life when travelling in Britain - clearing the table to wash up the dishes the moment meals were finished. This endeared him to miners' wives, particularly as stories went the rounds about the way he chastised their husbands for treating them as skivvies. He was the same at home: my mother cooked, he 'sided the pots' and he, or my sister and I, washed and dried them.

A SECURITY RISK

In the summers of 1950 and 1951, I spent some weeks in Czechoslovakia. Work and other pressures were beginning to tell on my father's health, and family holidays became breaks for rest and recuperation in Czech state sanatoria. In 1951, I stayed on there after my parents' return to the UK, living with Otto Sling and his English wife Marian. Otto - 'Uncle Otto' to me - was the Party Secretary for an important industrial region and he'd been a family friend when he was in exile in London during World War Two. A year later he was tried and shot in the purge known as the 'Slansky Trials'. On learning this, I remember asking my father what it was all about, but it was clear he didn't want to talk about it. I learned much later that he'd visited the Soviet Embassy in London at the time of the Trials to press his view that Sling couldn't possibly have been the British intelligence agent he was alleged to be, but his testimony was evidently ignored. Otto Sling was later 'rehabilitated', for what that was worth, and this was my first personal brush with the well-known 'excesses' of Soviet and East European regimes in which they'd devoured their own children.

I left school in 1953 when I was 17 and, after a brief spell as a butcher's boy, worked in varous capacities, from switchboard operator to invoice typist, at the head office of Colletts, the left-wing book chain. Most of my fellow-workers were CP members and I accompanied them on demonstrations and sold the 'Daily

Worker' at a lunchtime pitch in the Tottenham Court Road. I was reminded of the easier days of the wartime Anglo-Soviet alliance at the time of Stalin's death. The 'Daily Worker' headline next day ran: 'Stalin the Architect of Socialism is Dead' and I sold a lot of copies to people who normally never bought the paper and ignored those selling it. And in the days before, when it was rumoured that Stalin was ill, if not dead, quite a few folk asked 'How's Uncle Joe?', as if we had some special inside knowledge.

That sentiment was short-lived, of course, and for me was quickly overtaken by the difficult atmosphere of army life as I did my National Service. At that time - 1954-56 - military memories of the Korean War were fresh, and fighting was still going on in Malaya and Cyprus. I was half-way through my basic training at an isolated spot on the Welsh coast when my MOD classification as a security risk caught up with me. By then, having taken the IQ tests set for all recruits, I'd been interviewed and passed for officer training by my regimental selection board. This was cancelled, of course, and the appropriate officers and NCOs within my unit were alerted to the peril within. For my part, I was formally warned by my troop commander - a National Service subaltern with pink cheeks and little experience - of the awful punishments that would be visited upon me if I attempted to stir up the soldiery. From then on I was confined to postings within the UK and to activities distant from military secrets. There was comedy and paradox in what followed. For example, after my mutation from officer material to potential subversive, I continued to be trained as a radar operator in an anti-aircraft battery. The operator's manual was stamped 'Secret', but the gravity of the situation was reduced by the fact that the instructions printed on the set itself were in both English and Russian since the same model had been supplied to the USSR during the war and was, in any event, incapable of coordinating anti-aircraft fire against planes travelling at more than 200 miles an hour. I clung to such elements of humour as I could extract from these experiences as antidotes to the more unpleasant moments. Most of my service was spent in clerical work in a driver training regiment in North Wales. I avoided as best I could the attentions of those NCOs I had reason to think wished me ill, and I usually missed out on the Saturday night excursions to the pubs in Rhyll, the local town, since these could end in trouble in sidestreets or the bus station. On the other hand, my Battery commander and - crucially - the regimental sergeant major seemed to think I should get a fair crack of the whip despite my father's notoriety as CP general secretary and, ergo, self-proclaimed national traitor. I was promoted to Lance-Bombadier, a lowly enough rank, but one which provided me with a significant measure of personal protection, and I availed myself of all sorts of military and other hobbies open to me outside my office duties. I won trophies for rifle shooting. I was a member of the regimental athletic team. I picked up licenses to drive trucks and motor bikes. And I further fought off boredom by taking exotic courses such as one involving three days of intensive instruction as a hockey referee. Under the wing of the regiment's Education Corps sergeant, I went back to the set books of Shakespeare and Jane Austen and passed the Eng. Lit. 'O' level I'd failed at school for want of interest. Additionally, I topped up my pay by working three evenings a week switching the projectors, changing the reels and opening and closing the curtains at the 'Gaff' - the camp cinema. But my concluding months of service were pretty miserable, being mostly spent in and out of the camp hospital with septicaemia - a souvenir of botched dental surgery in Chester Military Hospital. When I was discharged in July 1956 I was run down, badly underweight and was still spitting out bone fragments.

TREATED LIKE ROYALTY

I left the Army on 12 July 1956 and 24 hours later was in the Soviet Union. My father was ill in a sanatorium just outside Moscow and I was sent there partly to relieve Johnny Gollan as his companion and partly to recover my own health. It was a sanitorium of the Soviet elite, at Baravikha. (Some 30 years later, this was where Yeltsin rested up before his heart surgery.) I ate and slept a lot; played chess with Yuri Faier, the blind conductor of the Bolshoi ballet; rubbed shoulders with prima ballerinas; and exercised by rowing on the local lake, keeping a careful distance from Kurchatov, the nuclear physicist, whose bodyguard patted a shoulder-holster to indicate his wish that my boat keep its distance. The respect with which my father was treated by everyone was very noticeable and, as the son of a personage regarded as the authentic leader of the British people, I was myself treated rather like a crown prince. Much the same had happened in Czechoslovakia in 1951, where I'd fished trout, shot deer and been introduced (by Otto Sling) to Klement Gottvald, the Czech President. I took it all in my stride but in retrospect these experiences not only contrasted with, but probably helped to nullify, the hostilities of a British environment in which my father was often vilified and in which I, in consequence, was sometimes abused. More important for me at the time was that convalescing at Baravikha meant spending many hours alone with my father, with an exchange of personal and political confidences I hadn't experienced before. In August 1956 he returned to Britain but first took me with him into Moscow where we stayed in the Gorki Street flat where he was usually lodged during his Soviet visits. At home, I'd been accustomed to leave the room if we were visited by someone coming to discuss a political matter with him. But on this occasion I was allowed to stay while he learned the fate of British party members who'd 'disappeared' in the purges of the 1930s. The tidings were brought by Nikolai Matkovsky, who in later years wrote a biography of my father that, in the best Soviet historiographical tradition, avoided discussion of the awkward years of 1939-41 by omitting the period altogether. Matkovsky told him that the individiduals in question had been executed or died in the camps but he was glad to be able now to report that they were 'rehabilitated'. My father asked, since it was now his task to convey this news personally to their families, if there anything else that Matkovsky was able to add. Matkovsky was obviously upset, and asked plaintively: 'What else can I tell you? That we are sorry?'. To which my father replied, heavily and pausing between each word, 'That - might - just - help'.

My scant, but in youthful CP circles of the time unusual, familiarity with some of the human tragedies of Soviet history - ascribed from 1956 to the 'distortions' or 'errors' encouraged by Stalin's 'cult of personality' - in no way muted my enthusiastic identification with the Soviet and socialist cause in the international arena or my conviction that 'history' was on our side. As a child I read widely and precociously and my views on English history at school were shaped less by classroom texts than by the reading I did at home where, for example, I empathised strongly with the young protagonists of Geoffrey Trease's novels *Bows Against the Barons*, *Comrades for the Charter*, *Missing from Home* and *Call to Arms*. In a more adult vein, I'd read and re-read A.J. Cronin's *The Citadel* a half dozen times by the time I was 12, and I was by then also following Upton Sinclair's hero Lanny Budd through his anti-fascist adventures of the 1930s and '40s. Stories of Soviet heroism and sacrifice, such as *The Story of a Real Man* by Boris Polevoi, or *How the Steel was Tempered*, enthused me as did more substantial works such as Sholokhov's *And Quiet Flows the Don*. In non-literary spheres, the family celebrated the Bolshoi Ballet's visits to London as triumphs of Soviet culture and in the Albert Hall we thrilled to the performances of the Red Army Choir. When Emil Gilels or David Oistrakh played at the Festival Hall, Beethoven and Mozart seemed to have enlisted themselves in the cause of socialism. And, in what for many must now seem a strangely inverted chauvinism, when sportsmen such as Kutz or Zatopek left British athletes floundering in their wake, this was cause not to be downcast but to rejoice. With my father I watched Hungary's crack soccer team - 'amateurs' to boot - thrash England 6-3 at Wembley Stadium in 1953, the event being portrayed as a victory of socialism over capitalism, and the experience being the richer because one star Hungarian forward was an Army major, and a central defender was a deputy in the Hungarian parliament. I recall yet more clearly sitting at home in front of a second-hand 9" TV set to watch the progress, through to the 1954 Wimbledon tennis singles final, of the Czech player Jaroslav Drobny. My mother's screams of support became increasingly hysterical as each match was won - but afterwards came gloom and confusion when Drobny defected and his name was never allowed to be mentioned again. In 1956, this was all repeated on a larger scale as most of Hungary's soccer heroes left for the West and the vaunted major of the socialist Army ended up playing his football in Franco's Spain.

STALIN'S PORTRAIT STAYS UP

All in all I remember 1956 as a very bad year. In the first place, my father's physical health deteriorated and, worse, this was accompanied by a process of political and psychological demoralisation which made his final years distressing both for him and for those close to him. His high blood pressure was treated with a drug with now notorious depressive side-effects. He was often in pain from a damaged spine. He'd suffered the first of a number of minor strokes. And, when I stayed with him in the sanatorium at Baravikha, he was being treated - with leeches and with remarkable success - for partial blindness caused by a blot clot that had impacted on the optic nerve. At that time he was trying but failing to come to terms with Khruschev's attack on Stalin at the CPSU's 20th Congress. His own admiration of Stalin had always been unstinting and he excused his faults - crimes was not a word he would accept - by speaking of the harsh complexity of the times and/or of the mistakes or deceits of subordinates. It's possible that he would have accepted Khruschev's critique had it been delivered by Lenin. But no other Soviet leader was of sufficient stature to change my father's view of Stalin as a worthy and indispensable leader both of the Soviet state and of world socialism. A portrait of Stalin (which I still keep, with other memorabilia) stayed on the wall at home until my father's death. On grounds of ill health, he pressed his resignation as CP general secretary on an unwilling Political Committee in 1956. It was put to him that the British party could follow the example of the French CP, where an ailing Maurice Thorez formally remained as General Secretary while he rested and gave his health a chance to improve. But he would have none of this and, with the pessimistic conviction that he was permanently incapacitated, he opted instead for a largely ceremonial role as Party chairman. Just over a year later, with his eyesight restored, and increasingly uneasy about the leadership route now being taken by Johnny Gollan, who'd been his handpicked successor, he sought to return to his old post. This time it was he whose request was rejected. I was then 20 years old and, after two years' absence from home in the Army, I was of an age where I could begin to appraise my father with eyes that were not entirely clouded by filial devotion. It is a great regret for me that it was precisely at this time that he became least himself. His public speaking engagements, which usually boosted his spirits, were restricted to one a month by his doctors. With unaccustomed time on his hands at home, he brooded and became increasingly morose, delivering himself of bitter judgements that flew in the face of what he'd previously said over many, many years.

At this time, I still had no clear idea how I wanted to earn my living. I'd been bored at school and left with three 'O' levels to which I'd added one picked up in the Army. But this hardly qualified me for university entrance which didn't in any event much attract me. For want of anything better, I applied for a job as a trainee sales representative and found myself selling margarine and cooking fat for Unilever. I began in Manchester in October 1956 as a member of a mobile sales team that worked its way up and down the country preparing the ground for the company's promotional schemes. This work went on for two years. I was good at it and, unusually for someone without a university (and more typically an Oxbridge) degree, became a management trainee. But it was obvious that there would be a clash between pursuing a managerial career in a giant capitalist enterprise like Unilever, on the one hand, and being politically active in the CP on the other.

My misgivings about the work were exacerbated by my father, although in an unexpected way. He learned from me in December 1957 that, albeit on a proper private mileage allowance, I'd used my company car to ferry around stuff for the *Daily Worker* bazaar in Liverpool. He was worried that public political activity of this kind could threaten my job. He went further and said that I'd finally 'got (my) feet under the table', should now 'make a success of (my) life', that 'this family's made enough sacrifices' and that I should leave the Party. I was deeply shocked, mainly because it was such a distressing manifestation of his own declining morale, but it forced me to confront the question of whether I was prepared to suppress, if not abandon, beliefs and activities that I'd been encouraged to embrace since childhood in order to pursue material and social success as a good 'Unilever Man'. I wasn't, but I seemed unqualified to do anything very different.

I buried myself in work to the point of becoming ill and then gave in my notice in the spring of 1958 and set about acquiring the 'A' levels I needed for university entrance. My father disapproved since I seemed to be giving up something solid for something vague and, on the basis of my school years, he didn't think I'd "keep at the books". I thought the latter would be difficult too. It had been five years since I'd left school, and I didn't like the prospect of attempting it with my father looking over my shoulder at home. An ideal solution was supplied by cousins who invited me to live with them and my father's sister Ella on a farm in Derbyshire. This made it easy for me to break with all my ordinary social routines and to adopt quite new ones. I used my savings from Unilever and a small grant from Derbyshire County Council to enroll at the Manchester College of Commerce. I studied full time and in eight months picked up the 3 'A' levels I'd wanted, together with an 'O' level in maths that I took by correspondence course. Eventually I applied for admission to King's College Cambridge.

A 'RED' AT CAMBRIDGE

By the summer of 1959 I'd received formal confirmation that I'd been given a place at King's, from October. My mother, who'd backed my attempt to renew my studies, was delighted. By that time, too, my father had come to terms with my departure from Unilever and was revising his views as to my diligence as a student. The key moment came during a visit home when I was covering sheets of paper with elementary quadratic equations as an exercise for my 'O' level maths correspondence course. He'd stood impassively at my shoulder while I ploughed through a taxing essay on the British constitution but when I began, apparently effortlessly, to fill my notepad with brackets and squared and cubed 'x's and 'y's - for him impenetrable and therefore difficult, 'real' scholarly work - he patted me on the back and said 'That's the stuff, son'. When I was actually admitted to Cambridge he was more ambivalent. This wasn't because I'd thrown over a managerial career for a university education that might turn out to be a chimera. It was more because university education could be a two-edged sword. On the one hand, like most working class CP members, he wanted his children to take advantage of the educational opportunities they themselves had been denied when they were young. Indeed, they might tell their children that it was criminal not to, and it was an argument he'd often deployed to stimulate or, more often, to censure my performance at school. As against this, young working-class entrants into British universities tended to emerge from them having shed both the values and the cause of the working class. Hence such individuals might improve themselves within the institutions of higher education, but the process could rob the working class of potential cadres. I understood him very well when he once remarked that he'd as soon have me a boiler-maker as a professor. (He wouldn't have said this, by the way, had the working-class occupation so counterposed been unskilled.)

In any event, I stuck to my books and felt the better for going up to King's with all the 'A' and 'O' levels I'd originally envisaged. I was then 23 years old and I took full advantage of the lavish facilities Cambridge offered for the pursuit of the most diverse interests. I supplemented funds from a state studentship by working as a porter in the Royal Free Hospital in London over the long summer vacations. I was doing this in the summer of 1960, while my father was enjoying a last hurrah on a speaking tour of Australia. He overdid it, became unwell and died at sea between Perth and Freemantle.

I remember very little during the weeks between his death and his funeral, but do recall the generally respectful obits that appeared in newspapers normally mentioning him only in hostile terms. I was in Johnny Gollan's office at King Street the day after my father's death was reported and Raji Palme Dutt came in clutching a bunch of these very obituaries. He was furious and declared grim-faced that: 'These papers all say that Harry was the only communist with a sense of humour. They lie. If a comrade tells me a joke, I laugh'. In fact, the national press chose to play up the contrast between my father and the stereotypes of their own invention in which British CP leaders were portrayed as cold-blooded fanatics who served without question an alien cause and a foreign power. But it was true that my father's twinkling humour and warmth of personality endeared him to many who disagreed with his views, and also disguised something of his political toughness. These were also qualities that over many years enhanced his effectiveness as leader of the British Party. In the 1940s and 50s - less so thereafter perhaps - the most prominent Party or communist trades union leaders were pretty formidable individuals. Most of them were substantial orators who, like my father, had served their apprenticeships as public speakers on the soapbox, handling stroppy crowds in parks or factories. Some of them had served time in jail. Men like Campbell, Dutt, Gallagher, Hannington, Horner, Papworth or Piratin were powerful, often idiosyncratic, personalities and as a collectivity were something of an awkward squad. My father's warmth and humour - part of a skilled personal touch that was both natural and cultivated - were potent solvents in conflictive circumstances, and difficult individuals could find common cause in their loyalty and affection for him, if not for each other. When he died, it was not difficult for me to push the less happy recollections of his final years into the background and to fasten instead upon better, earlier memories.

A MOBILE CAREER

In 1963 I went to Cuba, to begin post-graduate research into Cuban agrarian reform. I was married by then. My wife was Australian and from a CP background. When I eventually returned to Cambridge at the end of 1967, I felt myself in several ways to be politically 'semi-detached'. Firstly, I was steeped far more in concerns about problems of socialist transition than in the workings of developed capitalist economy. Secondly, whereas CPs in western Europe and Marxists in general tended to be preoccupied with the condition and cause of the urban working class, my primary interest lay in agrarian studies and in the nature and fate of the peasantry. Thirdly, for theoretical insights, I drew more upon the oft-forgotten, and usually stigmatised, writings of defunct 'leftist' or 'rightist' Soviet political economists (such as Preobrazhensky or Bukharin) than upon writers informing the thinking of most of my political colleagues in Cambridge. Symbolically, perhaps, my 'semi-detachment' was also expressed by the fact that when I read or wrote about my

Cuban or associated researches in Cambridge I often thought not in English but Spanish. Lastly, while I was in Cuba, my mother moved to Australia with my sister and her family, and this further weakened my ties with my British surroundings. None of this worried me. After the sophistries and 'class games' of social life and politics in Cambridge and the Union Society, Cuba had been a cleansing experience. Moreover, if my interests, experience and expertise were exotic, they were at least my own and had been acquired by hard graft in taxing surroundings.

I had no trouble in reinserting myself in Cambridge University politics for this was 1968 and students felt they could change the world. Unfortunately, the general rise in student militancy was not reflected by any significant growth in the CP's student branches. These quickly became both caught up and bogged down in the vicious infighting accompanying the Soviet invasion of Czechoslovakia. Moreover, at national level, the CP (and its full-time student organiser) had grave doubts about the 'soundness' of much of what was seen and heard in the emerging culture of militant students. Students enthusing about Trotsky or Mao could trigger powerful conditioned reflexes that closed off all avenues of dialogue. In Cambridge, the most difficult characters in the student movement were what we termed 'the freakers' - the 'revolutionaries' who mixed up anarchism and dope and who attended socialist meetings only to prevent votes and decisions being taken. But more widely on the Left, the Cambridge University CP was known for its sympathies for Dubcek's 'Prague Spring', for its hostility to Soviet intervention, and for its generally open approach to politics. In consequence it grew rapidly between 1968-70, recruiting quite a few students from 'International Socialism' - which at that time was far more influential within the student movement than the CP. I had no difficulty in becoming involved in the international concerns of students, of which the Vietnam War was the most conspicuous. I was also fired up by the jailing of six Cambridge students in 1969, in the aftermath of a turbulent demonstration against the Greek military junta. But I found it very difficult to empathise with more parochial student concerns: Cambridge University students were privileged young people, after all, and the passions rightly inflamed in them by international injustices and atrocities were not very plausibly channelled into campaigns against restrictive college gate hours and the like.

In 1970, Allende was elected President of the Popular Unity Government and I was invited to teach and research at the University of Concepcion, a bastion of left-wing academia in the south of the country. I arrived in Chile in the summer of 1971.

During the summer of 1973 the national political situation became increasingly unstable. When the coup finally came in September, the military occupied the universities, suppressing students, teachers and suspect academic disciplines alike. There was a ferocious purge of foreigners who'd been 'poisoning the minds of young Chileans'. The leader of the University of Concepcion's Young Communists was picked up in a raid on my house on the first night of the coup. I was detained myself, at various times and places, by the Navy - it was a misfortune that a Soviet ship named after my father had recently docked at the local port - the Army, and by the plainclothes and uniformed branches of the paramilitary police. My wife, who'd been teaching at the Department of Anthropology while researching Marxism and Pentacostalism in a nearby mining community, was also arrested. For two or three days we were held at the local football stadium at the same time. This was unfortunate for our children, then aged four and six. The different intelligence services quarrelled among themselves as to what kind of fish they'd caught, but there was plenty to annoy them whatever angle they viewed us from. After some weeks of uncertainty, we were flown out of the country as UN refugees.

At the time, it was better for us to go to Australia and we regrouped there for a while to explore alternative, preferably stable, conditions in which we could live and work. This was easier said than done and, in the event, the family broke up. I eventually settled in Glasgow, with a post in Latin American studies at the university.

DISTRUST OF NATIONALISM

Throughout this period I was, of course, aware that some folk thought I interested myself too much in international questions and not enough in national ones. They were quite right. I found it particularly difficult to involve myself in Scottish politics, especially when these turned on the issue of national independence. I'd spent years as a foreigner working in stridently nationalist environments - in Cuba, Chile, Nicaragua, and even Australia - and while I had no difficulty understanding nationalist sentiments, I distrusted and was alienated by politics overly shaped by a sense of national grievance. And I certainly failed the relevant variant of the 'Tebbit Test' by remaining entirely detached from the tribal warfare waged between Glasgow Rangers and Glasgow Celtic, keeping the faith instead with my childhood loyalties to Manchester City and Charlton Athletic. (In soccer, as in political causes, I seemed inclined to favour losing sides.) But I did feel a need to 'come home' in a general intellectual sense and in 1982-83 I moved to Cambridge for a year to work, in Trinity College, on the papers of Maurice Dobb.

Dobb, who died in 1976, had been Britain's foremost writer on Marxian political economy and his studies of the theory and practice of socialism, capitalism and development were influential at home and even more abroad. He'd been a friend of the family since the 1920s and my intellectual debt to him at Cambridge and after had been very great. In working to bring together his papers and, later, to organise them as an archive at Trinity College, I was in a sense 'paying my dues' and, since Maurice and Barbara Dobb had no children, I felt something of a filial sense of duty as well. Working through Dobb's papers was also to reeducate myself in Marxian social science and to learn much about the history of intellectuals within the British CP.

Looking back, it was obvious that as I grew older and moved physically and intellectually into arenas different from those of my father, the influence upon me of his life and times diminished. But I in no way linked this with any process of 'rejection'. His primary, lifelong commitment had been to the cause of the underprivileged. He'd been fired in this by the shocking inequalities he'd seen and felt during his childhood and these also fueled his loathing of the upper classes. I'd been brought up in different, softer times, culminating in my access to the most privileged of educational environments. It was in Africa, Asia and Latin America that I tended to find the keen social injustices that most angered and motivated me. My work on these was often 'academic' in nature but it also sometimes served a useful political or social end. I was glad, moreoever, that my research method commonly required me to get my hands grubby and to work in physical environments seldom inhabited by development 'professionals'. These not only made a good living out of the study of poverty but often avoided it altogether during what they euphemistically termed their 'fieldwork'. My dislike of this may have stemmed from the diatribes against corruption and hypocrisy that I'd often heard from my father. This is not to say that he was an ascetic. During the 1930s, he and my mother had once provided some kind of personal support to William Hill, the bookmaker. As a token of appreciation, Hill subsequently sent a parcel of goodies to our home every Christmas. After each and every Christmas lunch, as he smoked a good cigar and sipped a fine brandy, my father delivered himself of the same judgement: 'You've got to hand it to the bourgeoisie: the bastards know what's good!' (My private feeling was that while Hill may well have been repaying some personal debt, he was also probably laying off the very long odds against a socialist revolution in Britain.) What my father detested were not the good things of life but a system in which they were appropriated by people who didn't deserve them. Equally, he despised leaders of the labour or socialist movement who fought the workers' cause as a profession but lived high on the hog with padded expense accounts while they did so. He exhorted Party members to perform their daily work with diligence and quality, whether this be in factory, mine, office, school or university. For him, there was a practical as well as an ethical streak in this because the lazy, incompetent or dishonest worker, student or professional could never win the respect, and still less lead, his fellows. I found these beliefs validated in real life. In particular, during my years in Cuba, Chile or Nicaragua I was left in no doubt that one of the more corrosive forces gnawing at popular morale were the 'revolutionaries' who preached popular sacrifice on the one hand, while being indolent or corrupt on the other. Of course, the puritanical nature of some of my father's codes of conduct could make them a burdensome legacy but he leavened them with a rich humour that could be appreciated even by officers of the Special Branch. It was one of these who, after my father's death, recounted a misadventure while covertly trailing him on a London bus. He tendered his fare to the conductor only to be informed that it had 'already been paid by Mr Pollitt since he was the only one who knew where he was getting off'.

To this day, I feel uncomfortable with discussions of the CP's history that touch upon my father's role in such-and-such a period or event. I dislike it even more when his ghost is summoned up to support the ephemeral figures of this or that current political faction. If I am to be objective myself, I must purge all personal emotion and I find that too difficult. And others often judge or use him without setting him in his appropriate historical context, or even understanding the importance of trying to do so. But this kind of problem is familiar to all children of famous parents - it simply goes with the turf.

COMMUNITY AND CHAPEL

HYWEL FRANCIS / ANN KANE

HYWEL FRANCIS is a professor and director of the Department of Adult Continuing Education at the University of Wales, Swansea. He was brought up in a Welsh mining community and his father was a leading CP member and trade unionist in Wales. His family moved to Cardiff and he later attended university. He was on the editorial board of Marxism Today *and has written books about labour history.*

MINING ROOTS

My father was Dai Francis. He was born in 1911 and joined the Communist Party in 1936-37 at the time of the Spanish Civil War, and that was the reason. My mother is Catherine Francis and is still alive - my father died in 1981 - and she was born in 1914. They both came out of the same mining community, the top end of the Dulais valley where they attended the same school. They got married at almost precisely the same moment my father joined the Communist Party: December 1936.

My father had the political interest; my mother never belonged to any political party so in that sense we were not a traditional Communist family. Women tended not to be politically active in mining communities; there are exceptions but generally women played a secondary role.

My mother had her own political views and, if you were to ask her, she would describe herself more as a socialist than a Communist. I remember she said half-jokingly, on more than one occasion, that when they were voting in local elections she was going to be voting with her family, because there were Labour candidates in her family rather than Communist. I suspect she may possibly have voted Communist on other occasions.

My mother was the strong silent person who ran the family and my father was the one who was politically active. The trade union and the miners' union and the Communist Party were synonymous in that sense. For my father they were indivisible, he was a communist miners' leader.

He joined the CP largely as a result of his experiences in what was then the South Wales Miners Federation, and was influenced by the older Communists who he modelled himself on, people like Arthur Horner and Dai Dan Evans and Will Paynter, who were three major figures in his life. I can never remember a time when my father wasn't politically active or active in the union; there were long absences when he was away at conferences or meetings.

My memory of him, as a child, was of him sleeping in the chair, recovering from long days in the pit and then other meetings. He was a working miner until 1959 when he was 48 and he got a full-time union job as administrative officer, then he was elected general secretary of the South Wales miners in 1963.

Earliest memories are of him returning from a big miners international conference in Luxembourg when I was about five, and then on another occasion returning from the Soviet Union in 1952 having been on a South Wales miners delegation which participated in May Day. He came back - I was six going on seven - and I remember him saying to other Communists in the village, 'I was as near as that house across the road (about 10 yards away) to Stalin.' There was a certain degree of awe about it. It wasn't a normal family or a normal father in that sense. My mother's mother was an invalid, so we never really had the opportunity of having family holidays because she was having to look after her mother in the 1950s. The occasions when we normally had gatherings as a family were only when there were union conferences, so if we were lucky we could get two of them: one in early July and one in early September.

My sister was seven years older than me. When my grandmother died and we were able to go away as a family, it was to the conferences in places like Scarborough, Torquay, Ramsgate and Isle of Man. I enjoyed them - those were the occasions when we went away as a family.

CHAPEL VALUES

My early life was divided into two very distinct parts. The first was the period up to 1959 when we lived in a mining community in west Wales. The only social life, in terms of the Communist Party, would have been the *Daily Worker* bazaar in November each year; there were no party socials like London Communists had. There would have been political meetings I attended as a boy - I remember being taken to a meeting after John Gollan was elected leader in the late 1950s. It was a common occurrence for me to go with my father to meetings and I would have been aware of people like Willie Gallagher, I can remember taking him to the railway station with my father after a meeting.

The CP was very much part of the culture of the community and its people were not seen as strange, even in the Cold War period. There might have been occasional times when the odd remark was made against you, but there were lots of other children who were sons and daughters of Communists, or whose parents would have been sympathetic to the CP or voted for it. In our village a councillor on the Neath rural district council was a Communist down to 1958; there were always Communist candidates, Communists were in leading positions in the unions and in public life in general. I wouldn't say we felt we were different at all.

My mother encouraged me to go to a nonconformist chapel as a child and to Sunday school; my father never objected to that. The interesting thing about him was that he himself had a quite a religious upbringing: he had been a Sunday school teacher, but had left the chapel around the time he got married and joined the Communist Party. So with one step he went from being a Sunday school teacher to a member of the Communist Party - people will say of him that he took a lot of those kinds of values with him into the CP.

The culture of the CP in the valleys of south Wales was still very much shaped by that chapel background. Relationships with women were very puritanical. If you asked him whether he became an atheist he would never give you a straight answer. I can remember as a child asking him those things and he said things like, 'that's up to you to decide'. In your early teens you ask those questions and challenge parents, but he would never be direct in his answers.

I think he would have described himself in the same way as our local doctor, who was a lapsed Communist, and would have said he believed in 'honest doubt' and that it was never absolutely clear. He wouldn't have even been clear about being an agnostic. I think he rationalised it by saying it wasn't particularly important. He rejected the hypocrisy of those people who said that they were Christians in the mid-1930s; but he carried with him a profound knowledge of the Bible and of Welsh hymns. He had an incredible memory and was able to quote in speeches parts of the Bible or hymns, much better than ministers of religion themselves. That in itself was not necessarily paradoxical for Welsh Communists; there were Welsh Communists who were still active Christians: the most famous one was TE Nicholas who was a minister and also a member of the Communist Party as well as a poet.

There was much discussion in the family, and the community in which we lived, about the fact that my father not only left the chapel but he also never went into the chapel subsequently. When my cousin got married in 1957 there was great discussion as to whether my father would come to the chapel for the wedding - and he did come.

It was only on occasions of weddings and funerals that he came. Interestingly enough, people perceive me in the same light, even though I am a member of the Labour Party. There have been occasions when I have spoken in a chapel at a funeral and I conducted a service there at a memorial meeting for an International Brigader. I feel uncomfortable because people treat you as a vicar or something; invariably these are essentially Communist funerals, which I have been involved with subsequent to leaving the CP.

CULTURE SHOCK

The second major event in my life happened in 1959 when we moved to Cardiff and suburbia in what was really a middle-class area. I went to a secondary modern then a grammar school. It came as a great culture shock to me to even go to a secondary modern and find that, universally, people were conservatives, and it was rare to find even Labour voters. The culture in the 1950s of 'you've never had it so good' was one of self-satisfaction with their lives.

It was odd to find somebody who described himself as a socialist in the secondary modern school. That obviously changed by the mid-1960s. It was an enormous shock - even the teachers used to mimic my valleys accent and that was a kind of humiliation. I was brought up in a bilingual environment in the home and to find someone else in the school in Cardiff who spoke Welsh was highly unusual. There might be two or three others out of a thousand children in the school. Similarly, in the grammar school there might be up to ten out of a thousand. There was a hostility to the Welsh language, some hostility to the kind of social background I came from, and I certainly didn't need to announce I came from that background - my accent told it all, valleys and Welsh and proud of it!

My father became quite prominent in public life quite soon, and by November 1963, when he was elected Welsh miners general secretary by ballot, it was a big public issue - there was a lot of publicity about a Communist leading the South Wales miners once again. Children used to come up to me and say, 'I hope your father doesn't get elected'; friends of mine would do that, although by then I was 16-17 and not so sensitive.

I think it was people in the Communist Party who came to the house and asked me to join the YCL when I was 16; and I joined for no apparent reason other than it seemed a fairly obvious thing to do. I was slightly intrigued by it and I think it would have been through knowing people in CND. I was beginning to take an interest in politics in the wider sense, through being active in CND and anti-apartheid.

I admired a lot of what my father represented. I was conscious of the fact that Communists were special; and the people I was brought up to admire were people who had been victimised, been in prison, fought in Spain, and some had died. One of my earliest profound experiences was finding letters at home from friends of my father who had gone to Spain and who were killed; my father had kept these letters. He was secretary of the Spanish Aid Committee in the village and he had kept those minutes and kept receipts of money collected - that had an enormous impact on me. It was always in my mind that something ought to be done about their experiences; that is what my PhD was about and the book that I wrote called *Miners Against Fascism*.

My father was quite an emotional speaker and he could move an audience, particularly in his later years - in the 1970s after the miners had won back the respect of the movement through the big victories of 1972 and 1974, he became a patriarchal figure on the strength of his prominent position in that he was one of the key founders of the Wales TUC and was its first chairman, elected unopposed in his last year (before he retired). The last six years of his union activity were the best because everything came together.

I think it would be fair to say it was my mother who brought us up. It was recognised that my father was the wage-earner, he handed over the pay to my mother; she ran the home and he had a public life. He was supportive, but I can't say that he played a significant role in bringing us up.

There were certain standards of behaviour and expectations of us as children; education was very, very important. Although he never said I should not follow him into the pit, it wasn't encouraged, and I was expected to go on and get as much education as possible. He never made an issue of it publicly or privately. He would have been disappointed privately about the fact that I was not particularly bright. My sister was exceptionally bright. She sailed through her 11-plus and went to medical school when she was 17, qualified as doctor when she was 22. I was very much in her shadow and failed the 11-plus twice.

I went to university eventually and he took some pride in that. The fact that, coming from a mining background, my sister became a doctor and I had an academic career was due in no small part to quiet encouragement at home from both parents in different ways. He never forced his views on us and was always prepared to listen to other points of view. He was a pluralist before his time, and he wouldn't have demanded we think the same way as him, possibly because my mother was a balancing figure in the home.

The only time I can remember CP membership being uncomfortable was during the Hungary crisis of November-

December 1956. I read subsequently that the Communist Party instructed people to scale down their public activities in that period because they were getting into conflict situations. They still held a *Daily Worker* bazaar in our village but hardly anyone came! Later on they lost the Communist council seat they had and my own headmaster won the seat for Labour. That was an interesting experience. And I remember him coming to the house and asking my father to join the Labour Party at the time; my father just laughed. He told me afterwards about it and I think he was slightly flattered.

My father was a 'believer' in the Soviet Union. He used to sell *Soviet Weekly* in the village square on a Friday afternoon. He and I did a *Daily Worker* round in the street and we built it up from about eight to twenty between 1956 and 1959, when I was a lad of about twelve. I would take one street and he would take another. It was a social thing as well, because he wouldn't just deliver it and ask for the money, he would be talking to people about their problems; he would take an hour to do his street, I would take 15 minutes to do mine, and I would get a bit cross with him. There was another round in another part of the village and I guess they must have sold about 50 copies of the *Daily Worker* in our village. It was a small village of only 80 houses, so they must have been selling to every other house, and in addition to that there would have been regular daily buyers. As time went by I used to deliver the *Daily Worker* myself because he was away.

THE SPARTAN BREED

My father's political development mirrored what was happening in the party nationally in Britain. He would have supported the Hungarian position and been pro-Soviet on that; but in 1968 he was against the Soviet Union's invasion of Czechoslovakia and was against the invasion of Afghanistan. The earlier support for the Soviet Union can be understood, it can be rationalised; you cannot explain it away but there were reasons for it.

Communists of my father's generation and the previous generation were perceived as being somewhat special, like Spartans - Will Paynter described it in that way. They had to be better than everyone else, they should be beyond reproach and their lives were something that could never be questioned, in their relationships with women for instance. That was the model: that you had no extra-marital relationships, that you didn't drink, you dressed in a particular way, and you were not careerists because you put the party first, and you listened to what the party said.

People had moral, physical and intellectual courage; and what disappointed me in the late 1980s - I can't separate the party from the party within the miners' union, they were synonymous to me - was that when the coalfield disappeared it was almost as if the *raison d'etre* for being in the Communist Party had gone, because that was the main focus of political activity. There was a tendency for us in South Wales to be syndicalists.

At that time I was doing a fair bit of writing for *Marxism Today* and was on the editorial board and working closely with leading miners like Mick McGahey and George Bolton. In the period after the 1984 strike, the party potentially had a very important role to play, taking the anger out of the situation and trying to hold the NUM together. It could have been an organisation intellectually important to the movement. In the past the party had been strong and courageous enough to say things that were uncomfortable and difficult, but I didn't think the party was doing that in 1984 and afterwards. There was a need for a proper open political debate about things like the UDM and it wasn't happening. That was what I thought was missing. When people criticise previous generations I feel that the previous generations did have the intellectual courage to be grappling with those difficult questions.

That intellectual cutting edge of the old Communist Party wasn't only confined to academics, there were organic intellectuals inside the trade union movement and almost all of them were Communists. There was an ability to articulate problems and difficult questions in speeches and writings that people like Horner and Paynter had, and there were many other Communists outside the miners' union who were able to write - I think that has gone. It has something to do with the disappearance of independent working-class education. If you look back at *Labour Monthly*, for all its faults it was an extremely important forum for people in the trade union and labour movement to get into the discipline of writing.

When I went to Swansea University I wasn't particularly concerned about getting involved in student politics. But I got involved in the socialist society, student magazines and canvassing for the Labour Party and Communist Party. Politics wasn't anything new to me; I was interested in playing rugby, my future wife, and work.

The Communist Party and Young Communist League was a very good 'marriage bureau' and that is how I met Mair, partly through the YCL and partly through CND. We were both on Aldermaston marches in 1963-64 and we met then. We were both in the Cardiff branch of the YCL. I was the chairman of it and Marion Pearce, recently president of the NUT, was branch secretary. We were sent up to Rhondda East to canvass for Annie Powell and I met my future partner really for the first time then. We canvassed for Annie in Mardy and Ferndale. It was my father's task and my task on election day 1964 to drive Annie around; he was on in the morning, I was in the afternoon. We did the same in 1966. Annie did very well, she may even have saved her deposit; she stood in 1959 and 1955 and subsequently became the first Communist mayor in the Rhondda. We weren't expecting her to get elected, but it was quite enjoyable going from Cardiff to the Rhondda, where you saw 'real' Communists.

There was a lot of excitement about CND at that time as something dynamic and outside the traditional political party structures, with all different kinds of people like Quakers. The biggest experience was the daily one of confrontation. Because you wore a CND badge in school or on the street you were identifying yourself with a particular cause and people were challenging you. Political hostility from schoolteachers and more conservative families would confront you - if anything, membership of the CND resulted in much more confrontation than membership of the Communist Party. You learnt the skills of argument and discussion as a result of wearing a CND badge, but those skills were part of your daily life if you came from a trade union and Communist background. People who came from a conservative background were not really used to debate and discussion like that.

FAMILY MATTERS

Over Vietnam I can remember the shock of the different kinds of slogans: the party's line was peace in Vietnam, whereas the ultra-left line was Victory to the NLF. The change over in the late 1960s from CND marches to Vietnam War marches was a profound change, as was the argument within CND over the Committee of 100 and non-violent disobedience. Mair and I got married in 1968, and missed the big Vietnam march in Grosvenor Square. The interesting thing was that we married in September 1968, the week of the invasion of Czechoslovakia. In those days you didn't have a wedding party, so we had a wedding and wedding breakfast and my in-laws, who were members of the CP, organised this wedding party for all those not invited to the wedding. Mair didn't think it was an event for us to go to so we never went to it. We went on our honeymoon. But that evening there were arguments in the wedding about Czechoslovakia, with friends and family declaring themselves for or against. Invariably my family were in favour and their family and friends were opposed to the party line. They wanted to make a big issue of the fact that they were for the Soviet Union. These arguments tended to occur more with my in-laws; my father's views and mine tended to coincide. As time progressed, in the 1970s and 1980s, the differences between myself and Mair on the one hand and her family on the other became sharper: over the *Morning Star*, over the miners' strike, over the Soviet Union, over the historic compromise by the Italian Communist Party.

The era of 'sex, drugs and rock and roll' passed me by I think - well some of it did. It was more through my wife who was at art college. My own family and class background meant that I was trying to work those things out through my early life. My father's influence was profound. As soon as I graduated, the first thing I wanted to do was research on Welshmen who fought in the Spanish Civil War, which is what I did. Once I got that out of my system, I didn't want to enter academic life at all. I wanted to leave and take a job in the trade union movement, so I managed get a job at the TUC. It was a good experience but it was good to get back to the freedom of academic life and we returned to Wales in 1972.

Things I have done since are rooted in my past in a way: I set up an educational programme for the South Wales area of the NUM at the time my father was general secretary; I got involved in labour history; founded the South Wales Miners library; and helped to develop Community University in the valleys, those things are all rooted to some extent in the radical politics of my father's generation.

We have discussed this issue about morals now that my daughter is getting married and she is going to be living with her future husband before they get married. That was something that never entered our minds in 1968. I'm glad that it did work out that way. Mair was finishing her degree the following year and we decided the natural thing to do would be to get married rather than live together, because it would have offended both families. Although Mair's parents were Communists, there were certain rules, we weren't bohemians and they would not have been comfortable with something like that. I was very dutiful and conformist. I think my father was worried about me at one point because I worked too hard at school, I didn't go out or socialise. I got annoyed with him because he told my friends to try to get me to go out more.

I was a bit of a swot, and I think it was a cultural reaction to moving away from a small village to a big city; it was a big psychological shock. I didn't like the secondary modern and worked hard to get out of it. I was happier in the grammar school, partly because rugby was more important there.

When there were crises in the union my father would say, 'You have to recognise that the union is the second most important thing in my life', meaning that the first most important thing was his family. The party was also very important and my father wouldn't stand for any position in the union unless the party either supported him or asked him, it was that disciplined. When he went for the general secretary's position, there were six candidates, five Labour and one Communist and he was the Communist Party nominee. Some would say that the party had difficulty in disciplining him on other matters at national level, and at the end of the day he was his own man. He was described in Vic Allen's book on militancy among the British miners as a 'maverick'. He was a syndicalist in the sense that he was a Communist miners leader.

He would rarely go against the party line, but he would be suspicious of people who tried to impose the party line on him. For example, the 1972 strike when they had to settle, some Communists like Jack Collins wanted to stick out for ever but my father thought he was irresponsible. No-one could tell my father which way to go and he moved for the return to work nationally. But he would rely on the party for advice and guidance in a confidential sense.

He founded the Wales-Soviet Friendship Society in his retirement, so those things remained close and dear to him until the end, to my mind too much so because he was living in the past. He had been very active in those things in the 1940s and 50s and he was, in a sense, re-inventing the past and revisiting the past.

During the Hungarian crisis, although he remained loyal to the party, and the party miners remained intact - there were no major losses, unlike in Scotland - South Wales led the campaign to integrate refugee Hungarian miners, against the right wing in the NUM. The right wing were the first to condemn what was happening in Hungary but they were the first also to stop Hungarian miners coming into the country.

SERVING THE COMMUNITY

I suspect I have retained all my father's influence and not discarded much; I certainly wouldn't reject anything my father stood for, whether the good things or the bad. He was very much a patriarch and very uncompromising about himself. He was not very tolerant of people who were using the union for their own ends, and always saw it as a privilege to work for the movement. He had some degree of vanity as well; he enjoyed the community and enjoyed being more than just a trade union leader.

It may sound a little grand but that's how I have always seen it - serving the community - and I left the mining community against my will. I resented that and I set myself the task of getting back there as soon as I could. The only ambition instilled in me was to have the best possible education. One never thought about a career. It was assumed in our generation that if you didn't go down the pit, getting a degree would mean a job for life. That didn't mean going out of your class, just stability and security. I think there was a poverty of aspiration and the great achievement was to go to university; we were the first generation to do so.

We have three children. Hannah is away in Manchester. She is the eldest and is getting married, although she says she is going to come back and live in Wales. Dafydd is in Cardiff but wants to come to West Wales where we are. Sam, the youngest, is going to the local comprehensive. My wife would say I have not played as big a role as I should have in child rearing and it is probably true. It was a patriarchal family structure in the past - my father came first with his union/political activities - and so it was with me when the children were growing up. I was completing my PhD and writing books, and the family followed me to London to get a job, and back to Wales for a job and so on. It's only in the last few years that my partner has been able to develop her own career.

If I was having a family in the 1990s rather than the 1960s I would imagine it would have a more profound effect on me. There are different attitudes towards men and their careers and that whole debate is more fundamental and rooted now than it was in the 1960s. In the 1990s I suspect there have been changes with women in the labour force and at the family level.

We are financially better off than our parents, and life was different anyway in the 1970s from the 1950s and 1940s when we were being brought up. However romantically people might view the mining communities, it was also a narrow experience and a limited experience, and our kids will have much better opportunities. They were educated in the comprehensive system in the medium of Welsh. They had the opportunity I didn't have - and that was one of the more profound reasons why we moved back to Wales: to bring up children in Wales and give them the chance of learning Welsh.

I joined the Labour Party in May 1990 and my CP membership lapsed in 1988. I didn't join the Democratic Left. There was that 'respectable' period when I wasn't belonging to anything. I was emotionally not a member of the party from some time in 1986: all my closest friends were then in the Labour Party, there was no political activity going on the CP in my area. It was a wrench, it was a difficult one, and for a long period I was thinking of the previous generations, and how they might have viewed people like me leaving. But in the end it was irrelevant really, what they thought, because we were inhabiting a new period. The moment of joining the Labour Party was when the last pit in our valley closed; it was as symbolic as that. It was like an end of an era and closed the door on that period.

ANN KANE comes from a mining family in South Yorkshire. Her father Jock and mother Betty joined the CP in the 1920s. Jock was a miner who briefly worked for the Coal Board after nationalisation and was heavily involved in the NUM in South Yorkshire, later sitting on the union's national executive. Ann joined the YCL at school and later the CP at university. She has worked as a teacher in London for 30 years and still considers herself a communist.

THE PIT AND THE POLITICS

I come from a mining family and my father was next to the youngest of a family of about ten. Most of them were politically active, and practically founder members of the Communist Party. They originally came from Ireland to Scotland, and half of the family were born in Ireland and half in Scotland. They worked in the pits in Scotland, but after the 1926 general strike they were not able to get work in Scotland, due to their union activities, so they drifted south and eventually settled there, my father in South Yorkshire and the rest of the family in the Notts area, Derbyshire which is where my uncle was involved in further strikes.

I believe that at the time my father, Jock Kane, worked for the party and both he and my mother were students at the Lenin School in Moscow in the 1930s. They went independently and only met later; my mother Betty was also a communist of long standing before she knew my father. They met in Sheffield after my mother had returned from the Soviet Union. They married and after their first child my father went back to working in the pits - obviously you weren't paid much by the party, there was no money, there was no Moscow gold lurking around! I think you basically relied on the charity of other comrades to feed you and obviously once my father had a family he returned to the pits and got work in South Yorkshire.

There wasn't a time when politics weren't a part of our life, though I don't remember it having a heavy presence - we were just aware our parents were active. We were never bulldozed into it, but, because my father was an active miners leader, as kids we met all the greats of the communist party - Willy

Gallagher, Harry Pollitt, Arthur Horner, Will Paynter, Abe Moffat. Whenever they did meetings locally, they all stayed with us. The women in my father's family were all active as well.

After the war, when they nationalised the pits, my father was invited to have a job with the Coal Board. In fact one of my earliest memories of their political position was when my father resigned from the coal board because he felt he was too closely involved as an industrial relations officer. He felt that nationalisation wasn't really working in the best interests of the miners and, because of his role as somebody who had to get the miners to accept something less than they were asking, he was unhappy, because his sympathies and interests lay with the miners.

There obviously was a big debate at the time in the house, and presumably within the party, over this. My mother said she never agreed with my father having the job in the first place, but in the end it was decided that it was quite important to have people on the inside battling for the miners. But I think he found he just couldn't stomach it really.

It was a really well paid job; he ran a little car and in comparison to miners we were relatively comfortably off: to give that up and to go back into the pits was quite a big thing. There were articles and pictures in the paper about it. After he resigned from the coal board he went to China on a delegation, that would have been in the 1950s, about 1953, when I was still in primary school. It was one of the first delegations to go to China; it must have been about the time of the Korean war because I remember there was a little scare and we didn't hear from him in ages.

A VILLAGE PARTY

I was born in 1942. I've got brothers and sisters older than me, they were born in 1940 and 1938. In the pictures of my uncle Mick, after his release from prison after the 1938 strike, he is holding a baby, which is my sister. That was a big strike and there was a national campaign to get him released, involving people like Sybil Thorndike who went to visit and wrote to him in jail.

We were also made aware that our parents were politically

involved through things like hookie rugs, which had been made for *Daily Worker* bazaars out of odd socks and that kind of thing. They used to run whist drives, people used to come and play whist in the evening to raise money for the paper and my mum used to go and sell the paper.

My mum was always active in the peace movement and the party. I think it was a conscious decision between my parents, although her work was always secondary to my father's because, politically, working within the miners was considered to be quite important, and obviously, if you've got a young family you can't give up everything. She only ever did part-time jobs to supplement the family income. My father never really enjoyed good health; my mother said he was often ill. I remember as a child him being really ill - I think it was partly when he worked for the coal board because the anxiety of what he was doing actually made him ill. He did have ulcers, and stomach and chest problems in later life which I think must have been derived from the pits - they were certainly not improved by them.

There were several other party families in the village, and a small branch located within the village, which dwindled later on. At that time there was quite an active party, not a big one, but there were quite a few other families. We never felt any different from anyone else; my father was a very popular man, was very well liked and in fact when he died and the local NUM got a new banner for the branch, they put his portrait on the banner.

He was a very well respected man, very well liked in the village. Our childhood was just endless knocking at the door, usually people coming in wanting help - problems at the pit they needed sorting out, they'd been ill and weren't given their sick pay, they had a form to fill in and they didn't know how to do it. My memories of my childhood are of meals being endlessly interrupted: someone would be at the door and my father would always get up and speak to them, then take them into the other room whilst we finished our tea.

Locally, in the adjoining mining village, there were a couple of communists who became elected councillors - Bill Carr and Sammy Cairns. They were also miners, so the party in South Yorkshire at that time did have a kind of political presence in the community, and in some of the other communities, as well as their influence within the NUM. I think it was my father's generation, people like Sammy Taylor, Tommy Degnan who were all really active in the NUM at that time - who really brought about a change, as Yorkshire had been a very right-wing area; they are the ones that really turned it around. Arthur Scargill, who was in the YCL when I was in it, followed on from them but they paved the way, they had done the hard work.

I don't think we felt that their political activity affected us at the time. My mother was always at home, and she used to run the family, but she also did have to go out to work because miners didn't earn that much. She had various part-time jobs in a sweet factory, as an usherette, and in an engineering firm, unskilled work really which she used to take on to supplement the income. My father was often ill and even if you got any sick pay you were really on the bread line if you fell ill.

There were several strikes. My father was involved in a very big strike in 1955 in the South Yorkshire coalfield which again made us feel very aware of what he was about. It was national news, and he was dubbed 'Citizen Kane'; we had the *Daily Express* giving big coverage and several times he was front page news during the strike.

I don't think they got strike pay because I don't think it was endorsed by the national union, it was unofficial. There's always a debate about flying pickets and whether they were first used in the 1974 strike which revolutionised strikes by organising groups of pickets to travel around different collieries. In 1955 anyone with a car in South Yorkshire formed into groups and used to go around to other pits to talk to the miners there about getting the strike organised.

A CLOSE KNIT FAMILY

At school I never felt different from my friends. I didn't have many school friends whose parents were also politically active, on the whole they weren't, but the fact that mine were didn't create any problems for me. However, because 1955 was such a major strike in the area, and at the time I think all three of us must have been at grammar school, I remember some rather unpleasant comments from one teacher in particular.

Because the strike went on for so long, the miners' children were given free school dinners, so for the duration of the strike we had to bring in a letter asking for the dinners and had to stand up in class with it. I remember in a maths class I was the only person in the class who had brought in this bloody letter asking for school dinners and I remember the maths teacher saying he would have expected some of the others to be asking but not me, because he thought this strike was being organised by the communists.

He implied it was all my father's fault, and we shouldn't be getting the free school dinners, and I remember being slightly embarrassed by that.

I was very fond of my father and my mother. To me my father was particularly talented, very gifted, I just thought he was great, and our experience of people's reactions was not what we read in the paper. Of course in the 50s, at the height of the cold war, communists were supposed to be these terrible monsters, which wasn't our experience; our experience was that our parents were very nice people.

We were a close family, we still are, and my father's family were exceptionally close in terms of aunts and uncles, because of their experiences. After the 1926 strike, because they were unemployable due to their union activities in the general strike, they were turned out of the house they lived in because the houses were connected to the pits. My aunts were in cleaning or some kind of service; one of my uncles was ill and was carried out on a stretcher into the workhouse, they were turned out into the workhouse. They had no more money. They walked down to England looking for work and their reputations followed them there. They'd go on the next day but there would be word that these people were trouble makers and a job wouldn't be available. People in the different villages were told that if they gave shelter to these people then their job at the pit would be under threat.

Later, my dad used to say he had a soft spot for the Salvation Army, because it was a lady in the Salvation Army who was willing to stand up and say you are welcome to stay with me.

Politics was talked about endlessly in the house. I remember when I was a student we had Bert Ramelson to do a student meeting, and when we invited him back he said that I was one of the few students who had had a truly political upbringing. He remembered my father nursing me as a baby when they were having hot political debates or arguments in the house. So obviously it was always there, but my parents didn't particularly talk politics to us. We did have books and I suppose we were unusual as a family in that all three of us went to grammar school.

Our parents didn't have that opportunity - not because they weren't clever enough, just because there wasn't that chance - and they wanted us to have it and were willing to make financial sacrifices, such as paying for new uniforms. They always felt that education was very important, and as communists it was one of the things they were fighting for, for working-class kids to have those opportunities; but we were certainly never made to feel that we were better or different from anybody.

RELUCTANT LEADER

I think my father was a very reluctant official leader. The party always wanted him to stand for union positions, but, after his experience in the coal board, he was never really convinced of that importance, he felt it more important to be a member of the rank and file, that was the key thing.

My father was first elected in the late 50s to a union job. He was elected as an agent and was responsible for the pits in South Yorkshire, and then later on was elected as financial officer for the Yorkshire area of the NUM and he was on the national executive.

Most other people who were elected to the union, and people that have followed him since, moved out of their pit house, but we stayed in our pit house. The union bought houses and their officials often moved out - not out of the community since Barnsley is a mining town - but into houses owned by the union which would probably be a bit smarter than a pit house. The pit houses were just terraced houses, and for the most part of our childhood we had an outside toilet and we had those big black leaded grates in both rooms. There was a large kitchen, a living room, 3 bedrooms, a bathroom and an outside toilet. My father never moved away from our house, he travelled into Barnsley, where the union headquarters was, on a daily basis. He always felt it was important to keep those links in the community with the men who had put him there.

I think in many ways people would call my mother an old Stalinist. She was very reluctant to hear criticism against the Soviet Union and I suppose they were both fairly defensive of the Soviet Union, but I think on the other hand they were extremely open people.

My father got on well, for instance, with the local vicar, and particularly one who was responsible for the pit. They were like the early forerunners of a Christian Marxist debate, and in the local village a couple of times he went to a church group to discuss ideas. He was very open like that, although I don't think he had any doubts about his own convictions. Being Irish, they were a catholic family. His oldest sister has remained a catholic throughout her life, but you couldn't get a more staunch supporter of the party and the miners. She celebrated her 100th birthday last year and still retains her contact with the church. In fact my brother and sister were christened in the Catholic church, which my mum always complains about.

Her family weren't communists but her father must have been in whatever the Labour Party was called before. He was an atheist. So she had some socialist input from her family, but she was the only one of her family who actually joined the communist party. She came from an atheist background, where my father came from a strongly religious background. But most of them didn't pursue the catholicism - though Bridget did and another sister. Her children are very strong Catholics, but that didn't present a problem within the family - as I said, to please her, my brother and sister were actually christened in the catholic church.

My mother would not have agreed to say she would bring them up as Catholics, but the priest in the village at that time didn't seem to care, he just christened them anyway. I've not actually been christened, they wouldn't agree to christen me unless my parents were going to bring me up as a catholic. They weren't going to so they didn't bother.

The sense of unity within the family was never threatened,

and in fact they are quite an argumentative family. They have very strong views. One of my dad's sisters never joined the Communist Party but was in the Labour Party - she was in fact mayor in Stavely where they were settled. They had lots of vigorous debates about the Communist Party and the Labour Party and she obviously felt they should have been in the Labour Party, but it didn't matter how vigorous their disagreements were, they remained friends. I don't ever remember it causing an upset, in terms of the affection they had for one another.

YCL AND UNIVERSITY

I can't remember what led me to join the YCL. I joined while I was still at school, in the sixth form I think, and there weren't many others, apart from sons and daughters of other party members.

My brother must have been a student by that time and he joined the communist society at Sheffield University. One of my friends had a brother who was almost the same age as my brother, and she lived in Chesterfield, which is where a chunk of my father's family were. Our relatives were communists and they were often there when we went over to visit, and we established our friendships from way back then: so we all joined the YCL at the same time. My sister never had the inclination. She left and did a secretarial course and pursued that as a career. My brother and I went to university and I think my parents would have liked Pat to go to university but, in the end, if she didn't want to then there was no point in forcing her.

As far as holidays were concerned, we didn't have many, and that came later, when my father was a union official and we were grown up. I was at university when he became elected as an official, so in childhood our holidays were few, though we had one in Robin Hood Bay on the east coast.

We were looking at the old photographs recently - we didn't have good cameras but we had a tiny mickey mouse camera which took tiny photographs - and we were like matchsticks as kids. There we all are on Robin Hood Bay beach with our little knitted swimming costumes, sea up to our knees, and freezing to death. My father had negotiated with somebody to take us in the car to

Robin Hood Bay, and he was going to collect us and take us back. But he didn't turn up to collect us and we had to be out of the house we had rented. In the end we caught the train back.

I didn't go to Eastern Europe on holiday, but my sister went after my aunt and uncle paid for her to go to Czechoslovakia. My brother and I didn't go. Perhaps that was more true of party people in the south of England. There certainly was a feeling that the CP in the south was different. I think my father felt that perhaps some of the party officials took themselves a bit too seriously over theory and dogma, he was much more open minded about things. For him it was really theory in relation to his experiences of life, rather than theory for theory's sake. He certainly could intellectualise his position. When we were students he was often asked to come and talk to the students union, and the communist society would organise a meeting and that kind of thing. He was always invited to do things like that, and he could hold his own in that kind of situation.

FIGHTING FROM INSIDE

I think being a communist guided everything he did within the union as well, but I don't think he felt it was the party at all costs, right or wrong. I do know he occasionally had differences, for instance over standing people for union positions.

In Yorkshire they established a broad left and when positions became available my father felt very strongly that the broad left should decide who they were going to put forward. Often the party officials would want to promote another party member and I know my father at times had differences with the party leadership over that. He said you couldn't expect to work with people and then always presume that you were going to dictate who the candidates were going to be, and that they had always got to be in the Communist Party. If you were working in the broad left way they had to have the opportunity of deciding. I think on one occasion the party went ahead and stood a communist candidate even though the broad left had decided to support someone else. My father felt they shouldn't have done that.

I remember another incident in the Kent coalfield, where he

was furious. There was some kind of position coming up in the Kent union and two communist members stood for it. My father thought that was ridiculous. He felt that the party should have interceded to say that this was nonsense; so he certainly didn't feel that because of the work he was doing as a communist - I would say that everything he did was directed by what he believed in as a communist - that didn't mean that you always had to have someone in the communist party as a candidate.

You absorbed politics rather than had it directed at you, you were aware of what your parents felt rather than them lecturing you. I remember in 1956 a massive upheaval in the party as lots and lots of people left. Some of the people in the village left, and I remember a party convert from the village coming up to the house saying he wanted to talk to my dad about things. I thought this guy was talking to him because he wanted to leave; but in fact he had come to talk to my dad as he was concerned about another comrade who he said was on the verge of leaving, as a result of the revelations of the 20th Congress in Russia. I remember that bloke didn't leave but subsequently dropped out.

My father later said that he felt the revelations were terrible, and he had been horrified at had what had been done in the name of the party. We had had no knowledge about what had gone on in the Soviet Union, and the way it wasn't developing as we thought or hoped. He said there was no point in denying or making excuses, though he didn't think we should be totally negative about the subject, there were positive things there as well.

But my father felt that it was even more important to remain within the Communist Party to ensure those kind of mistakes weren't made again, we weren't communists to do that kind of thing, our ideas and aspirations were really against all those things that had happened within the Soviet Union, and that didn't change our ideals.

His generation came through the pits and through their experiences in Ireland. One of my father's brothers had a brief spell in jail, accused of possessing explosives for the IRA; it was in the 1920s and it wasn't proven and he was released. Their whole history is of struggle. They were really driven off the land in Ireland and suffered terribly because of the English. Their mother was very passionate about it in terms of justice and rights.

They were communists as a result of their experiences. They argued for the support of the Soviet Union. I don't think they were completely uncritical of the Soviet Union, but nevertheless they didn't go along with the general thrust of anti-sovietism and criticism of the Soviet Union, and it didn't make them any less confident about being communists. In many ways it made them more confident about being communists.

My parents accepted that the revelations were true but I think they also felt the Soviet Union had been battling against the odds; it wasn't all bad on that side, there were positive things as well. There was a sense of impatience within the communist movement rather than aligning themselves with one branch or another. My father visited China in the 50s, which was of course wonderful, and the initial effects of the revolution had very positive outcomes for the population.

That is probably how I came into the YCL when I was at school. We went on quite a number of CND marches while we were at school, I remember one from Manchester to Hull. We were in the local CND group. At the time of the Cuban crisis there was quite a strong communist group and within the group there were quite strong differences in people's assessment of the Cuba crisis. Some people felt that the Soviet Union was responsible, for participating in the crisis, whereas others of us felt that without the Soviet Union Cuba would not have existed. We can see now that the Soviet Union has collapsed and is not able to give any economic support to Cuba.

TURNING IN ON OURSELVES

I still regard myself as a communist though, I'm not particularly active at the moment. I still tag along to marches and contribute to things, as I think it is important that there is an alternative.

But I sometimes feel that we turn in on ourselves and forget the impact of imperialism which is still there in the world. I caught the tail end of a woman talking on television, saying they had huge quantities of the world's resources in Africa, but economically they were still being controlled by foreign countries.

Her hope was that eventually they would be able to take charge of their own economy - and you know the system is still there. We don't want what has happened in Eastern Europe and the Soviet Union, we don't want that kind of socialism, but we've still got to address how you are going to organise society in a way which is going to be more fair. It seems to me that that is what being a communist is all about, organising resources in a more fair and just way - and thinking how one does that without ending up with what happened in the Soviet Union.

The political set up we've got doesn't satisfy the needs of ordinary people. We've got a huge chunk of really dispossessed people. There is no hope of jobs, and technology has taken away many types of traditional work; it doesn't seem to me that a capitalist society has the capacity or the will to deal with that in a way that still makes people's lives bearable. Everything is driven by profit. I know we don't want things to be uneconomical, but there has got to be a limit to the excess of profit that is needed.

I am significantly better off compared to a lot of people I know. I work as a teacher, and I live with my partner, a pharmacist, he's got a shop so we are comfortable at the moment and we don't have to worry about paying our bills. I don't feel we lead excessive lifestyles and I just cannot imagine how other families survive.

NO TIME TO DROP OUT

Sex, drugs and rock and roll? It must have passed me by!

I had just started teaching in the early 60s when I first moved to London, but I think I had quite a strong sense of always working, that you worked. My parents had worked and it was obviously a hardship for them to put us through university - we lived off our grants but it wasn't easy for them - I don't think it would have crossed my mind to drop out of university.

I don't know how we would have dropped out. I have to say a lot of people that I have met who have dropped out actually had middle-class parents who supported them. They weren't drop-outs in society, they were paid for by their parents who could provide for them. I had a lot of friends who smoked pot, and I never really felt left out. I just lived my life the kind of way I wanted to live it. I didn't feel, because everyone was into that, that I should necessarily be into it. It would not have occurred to me not to work because what would have I lived on?

If somebody else is paying the bills for you, I feel it is very easy to be critical of things. I remember I shared a flat with someone who was in the party - in fact she was a very interesting woman, she had a brother who had fought in Spain and she was quite a bit older than me. She had a lot of nieces and nephews who were more or less the same age as me. They had a very casual lifestyle and rejected mainstrean values. They supported anti-Vietnam war demonstrations but were not aligned to political group.

I remember they were often very critical of people like me and my brother, who was also a teacher in London at the time, and I had quite an argument with the boyfriend of one of these nieces. They had dropped out, they weren't doing anything, had left school and didn't have a job. They would say to us that we were selling out because we had been to an imperialist university. They almost described us as class collaborators because we had been to university then got a job, so we were part of the system.

That annoyed me, considering he was living on a cheque that came from the States every month. The nephews and nieces had little private incomes from the investments their families made. If they got really stuck they could go home and their parents could afford to bail them out. Certainly, if I was stuck there is no doubt in my mind that my parents would bail me out, but I would never dream of putting that kind of burden on them.

My mother is 88. She got her first cheque book about three years ago, after never having one until then. My father must have been in his 60s before he had a cheque book, but he rarely used it. They only had a cheque book because when my father worked for the union they paid into a bank account. When I was in my 30s, my parents still lived in a miners house. The coal board decided to sell it and they had the option of buying it, and I think then it was going to cost about £1750. Even then my parents didn't have £1750, which wasn't a fantastic amount of money. One of my mother's sisters had a bit of money and gave my parents £1000 towards the house, and the three children - Mick, Pat and I - were going to chip in £250 each - for them to be able to buy the house they didn't have. My father was 70 years of age and worked all his life but he had to rely on others to secure his home. In the event my father died before they were able to buy the house. But if we had been in difficulty there is nothing that would have prevented me from going home and asking for help. We always knew we could go there, and my parents did help me out; but we are talking about small amounts of money but even then it was a sacrifice for them.

THE JOURNEY

CAROLE WODDIS

CAROLE WODDIS was born in Nottingham. Her father was a consultant psychiatrist and a CP member in his early years, although he kept his membership a secret for most of his life. Her uncles Jack and Roger were well known CP activists. She attended private school and then worked for the Royal Shakespeare Company and the Royal Ballet. She emigrated to Canada in 1966 and travelled in South and Central America. Later she went to Warwick University and became a journalist at City Limits *magazine. She is now a theatre critic.*

RE-INVENTING THE WORLD

We lived in Nottingham and my father Keith was a psychiatrist. He was from a Jewish-Polish background originally, first living in the East End of London then Golders Green. My mother's family came from Derbyshire and were Methodists or Baptists. My father's family turned away from Judaism when his father died; he was then 14 and the oldest boy of five. I was always aware as a child that both parents were nonconformist, and when my father married they wanted to break away from both their backgrounds and 're-invent the world' - that was what they talked about a lot.

It came from my father's idealism - although I didn't know where that came from. It was only later, after he died and I read his letters to my mother, particularly one sent after visiting Paris where he had attended a congress in the late 1930s, that I realised the excitement he had. There was this feeling that communism was going to create this wonderful new world, full of equality and happiness for people and a good standard of living.

He was writing from London - he must have been staying

with his mother in Golders Green. His letter says, 'I may be wrong but I think you will find I have altered somewhat through my vacation. I am fired with a new zeal and I am going to pass it on to you or die in the attempt. Together we could do a terrible lot ... why do you have to set yourself up in opposition to my ideas? Why shouldn't we work at them together? Just think what a difference it would make to have something in life to strive for that was bigger than you, bigger than me, bigger than both of us, something that burns down deep into your bones, that gives you strength and imagination and the courage of which you never thought you were capable, which gives a meaning to life where before there was nothing but a selfish search for pleasure, that helps you to feel in true relationship not only to present history but to all history. Can't you feel it pulsating within me, the hope and the certainty that if the millions of ordinary people like you and me would only take fate by the throat and strangle it, we can literally change the world?

'Darling, you know I love you with every atom of my being that is capable of love, but what sort of love is it when we have different ideals, when all the things I think are worth living for, for you are just so much eccentricity. Come out of your shell and forget about your romantic dreams and work with me to help our great-grandchildren to live in a world where the dread of war will be a bad dream, where man is no longer exploited by man, where all mankind will collaborate in fighting against famine, drought and disease and space and the elements and their own mind instead of spending the greater part of their income in preparing us for a deep destruction.

'You may think I'm crazy but after talking to Frenchmen and Englishmen and Americans and Scandinavians and Chinese during the past week I am certain there is only one thing worth a tinker's cuss at the moment. The key man to the whole world situation at the moment is our Nev, if he were forced to go the outlook would change overnight. That is not only my opinion it is the opinion of thinking men and women all over the world.

'It is so important that people in London are giving up their jobs to throw themselves wholeheartedly into the fight, people of every level in society, Conservatives, Liberals, Labourites, Communists, League of Nation Youth Unionites, Peace Pledge

Unionites, Co-operators, British Youth Peace Assembly, International Peace Campaign, the unattached millions, Christian Pacifists, all working, talking, thinking, writing only along one line: how to unite the mass of ordinary people like you and I into a great irresistible force that will sweep Chamberlain and all he stands for out of office. This will see that the people work decent hours, have holidays with pay, get sufficient food for their children, both employed and unemployed, see that youth is not forced into blind-alley jobs, break the hold of finance on the life of this country and collaborate with Russia, France and the USA to try and halt the aggressors and mad dogs of this world, who think only of the power of the class they represent and not the happiness of the people as a whole.

'You may think I am suffering from paranoia and have delusions but of one thing I am quite certain, and that is with or without your help I am going to work as I have never worked in my life to help such a state of things to come about and I shan't be alone at least in spirit in my endeavours.'

KEEPING SECRETS

My mother wasn't a Communist. She was a woman who happened to have in her an extraordinary mix of conservatism but also a very strong gut feeling for social justice, acute to identify humbug or the under-dog; and these things were constantly in conflict in her. For my father these were certainties, at that point in his life anyway. I didn't know until recently, when my mother told me - my father died about 13 years ago - that she thinks he was still in the CP when he was a doctor up in Nottingham. But he had to keep certain things quiet: first, the fact that he was Jewish: the hospital was run by a charity in those days before the NHS and if they had known he was Jewish they would not have kept him on the board - there was a lot of anti-semitism around. The other thing he kept very quiet was that he was a member of the Communist Party. They did have the odd secret meeting but he didn't even tell my mum about it, he didn't want to get her into any trouble.

When I was growing up I wasn't aware of any political involvement, but I was aware that the family felt slightly different. At school in the 1950s, when they were going on about Harold Macmillan, my parents were always very much against any conservatism. We always took an alternative stance to whatever was the prevailing established view. There were comments at home, but very quietly, and I never felt my father campaigned to win me over. I just absorbed it, like breathing in and breathing out.

Mum doesn't know when he stopped being in the party and I have no idea when he decided to leave. As it has come down to me, he said he acted this way because he did not want to be put under any kind of danger: he thought that if his Communist activities, or the fact that he went to meetings, were known, he would be out on his ear. He also thought that the less my mother knew the better. Clearly, she was vaguely aware that there were some meetings being held in the hospital, by people who perhaps were in the party, or sympathetic, in Nottingham.

As far as I was concerned, his idealism and his romanticism and the feeling that he wanted to create a better world - he lived that every day of his life, in the way he ran the hospital as a family. He was always known as a very liberal psychiatrist, and became known as the campaigning psychiatrist of the Midlands. He was one of the first doctors to have an open door policy.

He went there in the 1930s and it was then a very harsh regime. He ran the hospital along very humane lines for 45 years, and brought in a lot of liberalising schemes. He introduced groupwork therapy where that had never happened before, and he raised money to have a building completely run by the patients, where staff could not go unless they were invited by the patients. On his day off, Sundays, he used to go to Lincoln Prison and see murderers; he would go to court and plead on their behalf and try to understand the reasons they had committed the crimes. When he read RD Laing he felt greatly upset by him because it made him feel that what he had been doing all his life had been wrong: it challenged him on a very profound level.

He trained as a doctor at Barts and wanted to be a paediatrician; but had to get a job very quickly, with four siblings in the family and him the oldest boy, and this job in Nottingham came up very quickly. At the end of his life he always said psychiatry wasn't the job he had wanted to do anyway; yet he had spent 45 years of his life doing it. He always sent money back to his mother, he was very responsible.

He was an idealist in the way he treated people; no matter who they were, he treated them with the utmost respect. I saw the way he was with people; he just treated every human being with this respect, and that is terribly rare. When he talked about social deviancy, it was always to do with environment, there was always a reason and rationale; he didn't believe people were born evil. He thought genes were important, but the inference I had was that behaviour was more due to environmental factors.

He was a very good man. He lived out his Marxism every day of his life, even when he stopped being an organiser and began to lose faith in communism. He read hugely and widely, and had a very broad view of politics. What happened in the 1950s must have hit him very hard.

CUTTING OUT FAMILIES

I knew Uncle Jack - Jack Woddis - was international secretary of the CP. Roger Woddis, another brother, was a CP member - as far as I know, all the brothers, as teenagers, were members of the Communist Party. Roger was an anarchist, although it was a left-wing anarchism. We never mixed with their children though, because we were living in Nottingham, and my aunts and uncles were in London. To a certain extent my mother and father had cut themselves off from family and wanted to re-create their own world - my mother for her own reasons, in that she didn't get on with her father and left home at 17; she didn't like her own roots, in Derbyshire, so she felt they could create a new world by having nothing to do with their families - we were not encouraged to have anything to do with the others.

It has been quite a long, slow fight to bring the family together, on my father's side because of this odd thing in communism about somehow family not being important, your personal feelings not being important. It has come down to me through all kinds of communist friends that communism, at some level, at some point, did try to be impersonal, and did diminish the importance of individual families. Father, towards the end of his life, said he was more humanist than communist, and I think he did move from communism to humanism, which meant that no ideology should be bigger than taking into account individuals, and it should be a balancing of the two things.

When I worked at *City Limits* magazine in the 1980s I was with people who were much more ideologically left-wing than myself, with quite a lot of antagonism between the different factions. I got involved in alternative health therapies at a time when it wasn't yet called New Age; it was frowned upon by the left because it was individualised. I felt sympathetic towards alternative, complementary healthcare because I felt there was a need for an alternative to the NHS; I could see the NHS wasn't addressing certain personal needs. I knew the importance of collectivity in terms of strength. But it seemed to me there was an area of personal feelings to be recognised and to be heard, so there was a genuine conflict going on there. We were a collective and trying to work through that.

I think I was a slow developer. I had this middle-class upbringing from my mother's side: she sent us to private school and my brother Paul went off to public school, which is a strange equation. One can only rationalise, from my father's point of view, that in those days he came from a generation that felt that education was the key to all kinds of doors. His own father was working in a shoe factory at the age of 12, and worked his way up through scholarships, becoming a teacher through hard graft; so my father had great respect for education. He must have felt in his time that the best thing to give myself and my brother was education, and a large part of his salary went into paying our school fees. I went to a private day school in Nottingham.

My mother's mother had some strange ideas, and wanted upward mobility for her daughters. When she knew my mother was involved with a Jew she raged at her and said, 'Get out of this house if you are going to meet that Yid again'.

What my mother does have in her, to this day, is a great sense of style and concern for appearance. She was always a great stickler for fashion, and she wanted me to be married, to marry well. I was offered two choices when I left school: go and do a domestic science course in Edinburgh, or go to finishing school on the Continent. So I was sent to finishing school in Switzerland for six months, which did me no good whatsoever, although I had a lovely time skiing.

After that I went to secretarial college in London, and I left home at 16. I got a job at Rank films. As a child I had been obssessed with two things, cricket and films, and we went to Trent Bridge to watch the Bedser twins play for England against the Aussies. Dad was a great athletics fan and took us off to athletics meetings, so I was very sports-minded. Finally I got the theatre bug and joined the Royal Shakespeare Company at the Aldwych when I was 19. By that time I had fallen in love rather heavily with my boss and had to leave; then I worked with the Royal Ballet before emigrating to Canada in 1966. I arrived in Canada just when the anti-Vietnam movement was starting; the draft-dodgers were coming up to Canada and I began slowly to get politicised.

It was as if all the groundwork my father had done over the years began to bubble up to the surface. I met quite a few of the draft-dodgers in Canada and the USA, then I travelled - in Central and South America. I came back a completely different person. I was angry with my parents, thinking they were very bourgeois and I felt terribly guilty - a guilt I have carried for a very long time.

A SLOW AWAKENING

My father absorbed it and, no matter how much I ranted and raved, it just got absorbed. Then I went to Warwick University in 1969, when EP Thompson was there and there was more political agitation. It has been a very slow process. I began to get feminism in the 1970s. My mother had always said she was a feminist, and in some ways she was, although she wasn't always sure what that meant. For her, feminism was just being anti-male, I think she saw it in terms of herself rather than it being part of a movement involving other women.

I worked at the Royal Ballet, the Royal Opera House and finally found my way to *Time Out* and *City Limits*. I remember having arguments at *City Limits*: people talked about when the revolution would come, and I was always asking about people *now* - there was, for me, always conflict between the long-term and trying to meet people's needs and hopes now, not in the future.

There were parts of my father that were deeply subterranean, to do with being in the CP, to do with his Jewishness, parts which he chose to suppress - which made for some difficulties with the family. My brother felt he was a very distant father. There was no doubt that he loved us both hugely but he wasn't always able to show that. He showed it in the money he put into our education; he never had any money for himself at all. To many people he was a kind of guru figure because he was so calm and so wise and read so much.

If he had been able to have been a little bit more open in all kinds of different ways it would have been a help; there is a kind of mystery there. In the last few years I have been analysing what went on. I have had little bubbles of anger, but slowly you come to realise that he did the best that he could. He was beaten up by the Brownshirts in the East End at one point, and I think it obviously pushed him further into himself

Ambition has been very difficult - Dad, perhaps more to do with his Jewishness, always felt it was terrible to push yourself forward, and he never would, which used to drive Mother mad. That has come down to me in a way. He was always very retiring in terms of material things, and in his career he was not very pushy at all. What has been bequeathed to me is this sense of altruism and responsibility for others, that we are linked in to each other; and it has sometimes almost pushed me to breaking point. I felt it was my responsibility to stop some of the evils of the world; and it became bigger as the years have gone on and I became politicised. Now I think I am letting this burden go because I just can't carry it. But in the last twenty years I have tried to fulfil the legacy and inheritance I was given.

Feminism was such a huge thing for me. I was such an evangelical for about ten years. Then I became a gay woman, and all of that was part and parcel of coming out from underneath. One thing led into another, particularly after Central and South America, but perhaps even earlier, because of my upbringing and the things I imbibed. I see it as stripping away layer upon layer and gradually discovering myself. Now I am going through another phase, where some of the burdens are being put down, and I feel in a little bit of a vacuum at the moment.

One of the things I admired about my Aunt Margaret, who died last year, was that I don't think she ever lost her faith in the CP, but she managed to transfer it into progressive politics of the now: she was very feminist in a quiet way and was always so supportive of me when I talked to her about my difficulties of being a gay woman. She was always there for me in her own way, as well as constantly being involved locally in CND issues and environmental causes.

ASKING THE QUESTION

MARTIN JONES / MIKE POWER / MARTIN KETTLE

MARTIN JONES was born in Liverpool. His father, who was active in the CP, took the family to live in Halle in the German Democratic Republic in 1959. He went to school there but was able to visit England because he had an English passport. After training as an electrician he switched to being a musician and formed his own rock band which was very successful. He now works as a radio presenter and lives near Hanover.

LIVERPOOL TO THE GDR

Right from when I was three or four years old I heard the words socialism and communism. I never really came to ask my father why he left England and his background and comrades. He probably wasn't happy with the role of the English CP at that time and the way things were turning out, because he was a Moscow hardliner. He probably thought that to proceed further you really had to leave Britain. Maybe that was one reason, apart from the fact that he did not get the job he thought he deserved. My mum was not very much involved in politics.

My father was in the army and shortly after the war he was sent to northern Germany to a telecommunications point; the German navy had a centre there. My mum, who is German, was his secretary and that is how they got to know each other. By the end of 1946 and the beginning of 1947 he was demobbed. They stayed in contact and a couple of years later they got married and she came over to England. She had previously been engaged during the war and my brother Achim was born in 1944. I think his father got killed. Keith was born in 1952 and I was born in 1956 in Liverpool.

My father, in the 1950s, was several times in Berlin, I believe, and there were others there already. He had gone on summer courses so he had contacts there. He really wanted to go to Berlin to the university, but things didn't work out. Someone suggested he went to Halle because there was a vacant job there, so he went there and that is how we got sent out to Halle. I was three years old and I can't remember anything about the move. Shortly after that I went to the nursery in Halle and started at school.

I first realised that the GDR (German Democratic Republic) was different when Mum took me to West Germany to see her relatives, and I found out they had fruit, they had chewing gum, they had coca-cola - they had nothing like that in East Germany. They had comics, but that was seen as American-capitalist culture and decadent in the east.

In the 1960s life in East Germany was rather poor. My brother Achim was a rock and roller because that was very popular, but he was forbidden to wear blue jeans. He wore these new blue jeans in the street, and the police told him to take them off - there were a lot of police walking around on patrol. Everything was controlled. The longer the GDR existed, the more these benefits about no unemployment and childcare facilities got worn out, because people had the opportunity to look over the fence through West German TV and radio. Pensioners were allowed to travel to the west and brought information back, and everyone knew the standard of living was higher.

Towards the end of the 1960s they established so-called Inter-shops, so that GDR people who possessed Western currency were allowed to buy Western goods. The funny thing was that most of the luxury goods which they could buy were produced in the GDR, and then exported to the west. This caused several questions in people's minds like, 'Why can't I buy these goods from the money I earn,' and, 'Why do I have to convert GDR marks on the black market to Deutschmarks in order to get anything.' The quality of the goods you could buy in East Germany was very poor. My dad always ignored it, because he saw it as propaganda: it was only a way to get hold of Western currency.

FOLLOWING THE LINE

At school we were told several times a day about the advantages of Communism and socialism, and that everyone has to proceed according to the line and the plan, and every different opinion is an advantage for capitalism. My father took a hard line on this and after the Prague Spring and the invasion of Czechoslovakia I dared not discuss anything like that with my dad because he saw it was a threat to communism; also Solidarity in Poland - any different movement was 'counter-revolution'. My father believed any material that came out of Russia or the Soviet Union: he was so hardline he was blind really. He saw everything through rose-tinted glasses.

We asked our mum about life in England: what was it like, did she suffer discrimination when she went to Britain after the war? And she said there was nothing like that and she was accepted right from the beginning. She remembers that as a very positive experience. When I asked my father why he moved to Germany, he said that because he was a Communist he did not have a proper chance to develop his profession in England and would have had to stay a teacher forever. I am not sure if that was an excuse; he was probably isolated in the CP because he was a hardliner.

My mum was interested in politics but she had different opinions. She said, 'How can you separate a country, how can you split a country? You can't do that'. She had to do all the shopping, she brought us up, my dad never gave a hand.

My mum became very, very ill with diabetes and she had to stay for several months in hospital. What did my dad do in order to continue his work? He put us in a children's home. I was a very young five or so, and Keith nine or 10. It was a home for motherless or parentless children. It was a terrible experience and we were in for a couple of months. He just got rid of us; he came once a week or so to visit us. I could never understand why he did that. He didn't know how to handle a household, and he was writing his doctorate, and of course he would not give that up.

My parents' discussions always ended up in rows. Kathe might have a different opinion about shortages, etc. He would not try to explain, he went up the wall and told her off. Most of his life he went into his room. He did a lot of translation as part of his university job, and when he retired, he joined the Institute of Marxism-Leninism in Halle.

We had a kind of political lesson at school called Citizenship, to teach children the basics of communism and Marxism. We were told that capitalism was chauvinistic and trying to exploit labour, while it was good in East Germany and the Soviet Union was a brother of GDR. There was a joke about this: 'You can choose your friends but you can't choose your brother, can you?' The Soviet Army was in the GDR and they were very visible on patrols and lorries; there were masses of troops - although they were isolated and did not have much contact with the population.

Dad used to ask Keith what he learnt at school; Keith said that we were told that the most important thing about socialism was the people, but he got the impression that socialism as a system was seen as more important than the people. My father nearly tore his head off at the evening meal about it, asking how he could be so ignorant.

I was sceptical right from the beginning. I wasn't left at all. I had been to West Germany, and my mother brought me to England, and I saw how people lived. As a child you first think about the material things you can have. I became schizophrenic, more or less, and my performance at school was very poor. It always puzzled me: why is the system like this and the other system like that? I never questioned things with my father because I knew it would turn into a row which would affect my mother.

He was very loyal to the Soviet Union and thought everything Moscow said was right. He was not a Communist, he was really a Stalinist, that was my opinion. Anything about the purges and what Stalin did was propaganda, it never happened. There must have been a few reasons for the camps, the Gulagsm, but I never spoke about it, I didn't dare. One day I might ask him the big questions: why have you changed our lives and ruined a part of our lives? I don't mind him doing it with his life, but he pulled us in.

He never said how he got into politics, just that his family was very, very poor; he loved his father, and his father left the family, and he had to take care of the family. He was very fond of his sister, Eve, and he had to raise money for the family. He did a good job in that and saved the family probably. My father has a very good brain in his subject, but he is absolutely disabled in tackling things in normal life.

TO STAY OR GO

I wanted to leave Germany when I was 18 or 19. My cousin Norma got married to Ken, and they came and stayed here. Then I came over with my mum. I had nearly finished my apprenticeship as an electrician and was going into music and I had this idea in my head of becoming a musician in England. I always thought I wasn't good enough or professional enough, and I realised later that these thoughts came from my dad.

Keith did get out of it, and started to develop his own mind after he left. We both talked about getting out, but we did not want to leave Mum alone. It was easier for Keith because he was a doctor by then. He eventually left in 1982-3. As soon as dad became aware that Keith wanted to leave he tried to prevent him going. Keith would never have had a chance to start a real career in the GDR and would always have stayed a doctor at low level because he was a foreigner from a capitalist country, and not a member of the Communist Party. If you were active in the CP you would have a good chance to get on, but Keith didn't want to do that, and felt he had nothing in common with the system. He and his wife decided to leave the country, as soon as my father heard about this he tried to interfere and torpedo his plans. He went to see the ministry of health and kicked up a row; and that reflected back to Keith at the clinic.

This led to the complete isolation of Keith in the hospital: my father scored an own goal because Keith had to leave, he had no choice. They told the authorities they were leaving for England but in fact they left for West Germany. This meant his wife was not allowed to visit East Germany again and see her parents as a punishment, she only saw her father again in Prague. Keith was encouraged before he left to tell my father off and told him he must not interfere with his life anymore.

There was another occasion when I stood up to him - he

wanted to get a divorce when I was 24, in 1980. He said he wanted to find someone who agreed with his views. He shouted at me. Something boiled over in me and I kicked up a row with him for the first time. I gave him a 10-minute solo in which I brought up everything, and it all came out: the way he treated mum, and his attitudes, and he could not treat me like that anymore. And since then he tried to keep away from me and accepted my comments.

He isolated himself more and more. He only had a few friends such as an English couple who lived in the GDR. They had an organisation called the English-American Teachers Society and they had an annual meeting. He also had a few friends who were lecturers in Halle.

MUSIC AND FREEDOM

Achim was a rock and roller and Keith was a Beatles fan. I was a great fan of the Beatles and the Stones, what they called 'beat music', and we saw a monthly programme on West German television called *Beat Club* - and that was my education. The GDR government and the youth organisations realised there had to be something to attract the young people and the easiest thing was music. There was the World Youth Congress in Berlin in 1973 and that was a great cultural change; after that a certain kind of music started and rock and roll was allowed and used as a way to attract the youth. They established mobile discotheques so there would be a meeting of the youth group similar to the YCL, and after that they would have a party with a disco or with a band and everyone would stay, of course, and that is when I started playing music, in 1973.

I was in a school band. I taught myself guitar; Keith had guitar lessons so I asked him to show me a few chords. The music gave us a certain kind of freedom - if you allow a certain amount of freedom you probably have a chance to attract people again. They found out that there were very progressive kinds of music in the West - black music, left-wing music, folk music - and certain groups were allowed into the country, because they had to entertain the people. I formed my own band and went professional, then toured the country.

Music was one of the few ways to express yourself and to have fun; sport was probably the other, although you were welcome not just to take part but to get good results. Many medals were won by the GDR in swimming and athletics, but it took a lot of money and there were extra schools where people were trained and had school lessons as well. Only the best were allowed to travel. I knew, if I wanted to start a music career, it would be much more difficult in the West, but once you got going in the East it was not too bad. I had 15 gigs a month. We had a person who organised us, a manager, and we got a contract with radio and made several recordings of our own material. You had to have someone friendly to you, like a music editor or DJ, to get your songs played.

THE MAN FROM THE STASI

In 1980 or 1981 I got a call to go and meet someone who said he was an old friend. He turned out to be from the Stasi, the secret police. This was just after the so-called NATO agreements in which the West German government agreed to the stationing of nuclear cruise missiles. There was a big campaign against that, although no-one was talking about Russian rockets based in the GDR, because that was defending socialism while the other was attacking socialism.

The man was from the branch responsible for spying in foreign countries, and they wanted me to move to England and try to find people who had sympathetic feelings, not necessarily communist or left-wing, but sympathetic to the socialist system. They gave me a fortnight to think it over. They wanted me to live somewhere in the north of England so I would be away from the family. I think I would have had to report names, or mention a few names to them, so they would start recruiting, although I don't really know.

I thought about it. I would have had to break up my relationship and leave Germany immediately. I did talk about it with my girlfriend, who is now my wife. I could have told them right from the beginning thast I was not interested, but I was interested about this, what was it all about? Eventually, after another meeting, I told him I was not the right person and I would rather stay and continue with my music.

By the end of the 1980s, economically, the GDR was down to

the ground; everybody knew that but the hardline Communists tried to keep up the pretence. There wasn't much work or materials so everybody went to work in the morning but didn't have much to do - it was a kind of unemployment.

An opposition started, but once people had a different opinion and came together they were criminalised. I sympathised although I wasn't involved in it.

I did go to demonstrations in Halle in September 1989. It was in the evening in the market square and suddenly there were lights flashing and we saw cameras - the Stasi was filming us. There were groups of men - you could smell they were secret police - standing together in little groups, probably with the intention of starting a provocation, but they didn't have a chance because everybody brought children with them.

In October, on the occasion of the 40th anniversary of the GDR, there was supposed to be a big demonstration in Leipzig, and everybody knew the military would be there and clashes were expected. My wife Suzy, who is a doctor, worked in the department dealing with blood donations, and they were ordered to get all the blood reserves out: there was something happening I think that was the last attempt by the government to do something.

But Gorbachev was there then and there is speculation that he told them, 'Don't shed any blood or our reforms will be jeopardised'. That same year in June there was the so-called 'Chinese solution', the massacre of students in Peking. And we were close to something terrible happening, which I think would have started a civil war. Later on they interviewed people in the armed forces and they said they would not have done that; even police said they would not have gone that far (although there are always a few jerks who would have done it). There was an episode in Dresden where there was a demonstration guarded by police with shields and helmets, and a lot of the police laid down their shields and helmets and marched with the demonstrators. They were arrested.

END OF THE 'CONCRETE HEADS'

It broke down when Hungary opened the border with Austria in the summer of 1989 and loads of people just walked across the Iron Curtain: a mass movement started, especially among the youth. They went to Budapest - most of them went just for the fun, although no-one knew what would happen. Would Hungary be invaded again by the tankies, the Russians? At that time Gorbachev was in power, it would not have happened if Brezhnev had still been in power, definitely not. That summer I was in England with the family.

The GDR government was paralysed and did not know what to do. These tired old men - like Honecker, the party leader, who was known as 'concrete head' - they could not close the GDR down again because a lot of people also moved to Czechoslovakia and fled into the West German embassy there. The country crumbled. The demonstrations started in the big cities and then Gorbachov came to visit in October 1989, and he was seen as the Messiah. Reform would have meant to the old concrete heads that they give up power and open it up to democracy, because the GDR was never democratic in any sense, always it was run by Moscow hardliners.

When the Berlin Wall came down we felt a kind of relief, although no-one talked about re-unification at that stage, that came later. I had gigs over that weekend; then on the Monday the band went down the motorway to Hanover in the West. I never thought it would happen and that I would take part in such a great change.

Socialism as theory is probably brilliant and is a solution for, say, Russia at the turn of the century. Socialism is probably the only way for people to survive in that situation. Society keeps on developing and capitalism can only survive by changing, whether to more democracy or more dictatorship - it has to decide which way to go. Maybe one day there will be a fusion and, because I have lived in a socialist country and now I live in a capitalist society, I might know a little more than the citizen of a capitalist country. In the GDR women could go to work, there were plenty of nursery schools and creches - although you have to decide whether it is wise to give a child at two months away to a creche - but women were kind of free. The state paid for education and social security.

I never wanted to get married because of the way my parents' relationship turned out, but as I grew older I found out it is not your parents that make your life but yourself, and there may be a person you want to spend your life with - I wouldn't call it a partnership but a symbiosis. With my children, because of my experience, before I start yelling I think, is it really necessary? If I have to, I try not to hurt anyone's feelings. That is one positive effect from my father at least! Children are people as well and you must avoid anything that harms their personality.

Martin Jones is Phil Cohen's cousin and his father was brother to Eve Cohen, the author's mother.

MIKE POWER was born in Deptford, south east London and now works for the TUC. He left school at 15 and worked his apprenticeship in the print industry. He became a leading figure in the YCL and was a member of its national committee. Later he stood as a CP candidate in local and parliamentary elections. He went to university and then became a journalist.

A VICTIM OF WAR

My parents both came from Deptford in south east London. My father was born in 1912 and my mother in 1911. They were married in 1936 and more or less at the same time joined the Communist Party. Both had a real political awareness of what was happening in Spain and the anti-fascist struggles in this country.

In Deptford there was a famous Communist called Kath Duncan who, since the party was founded, had been a leader of the unemployed and housing struggles. She was a silver-tongued orator and used to speak in Deptford High Street every Saturday night and they all used to go and listen to her.

My parents joined the CP at this time. My mother was a secretary and my father was in the printing industry and a strong trade unionist. My brother was born in October 1939, and then my father went into the army - those three years were the only married life they had.

When the Second Front came in 1944 my father was a lance-sergeant in the Royal Artillery and he was doing troop training. He wasn't designated to do anything else and he was 31, which was considered too old for active service. But because of the party line of 'open the second front' he volunteered to go, which didn't seem very sensible, given they had a four-year-old son and my mum was six months pregnant with me - but that was the line. Being in the Royal Artillery he was in the first wave of Normandy landings, so they took the brunt. He went out on July 8 and eight days later he was dead. He is buried in Normandy, and the gravestones around him are all 18- and 19-year olds.

To have been a communist in Britain in the late 1930s when the party was relatively small, you had to be deeply questioning of your own society; but then people became unquestioning about the alternative, which was modelled on the Soviet Union - that was the problem. A lot of them became people who loved humanity so much, with unbelievable commitment to the people, the masses and humanity, but they had no time for individuals or their home lives. It was absolutely ludicrous: in my family it meant that my dad insisted on going to war, leaving behind a wife and a four-year-old, with me born three months after he was killed. The party wasn't a prison, people could leave and join, so in that sense people had free will. But once you were in, the expectations and the discipline were quite strong.

My mother was evacuated to Somerset where I was born in 1944; then she came back and lived with my grandparents. In 1945, when I was barely a year old, Kath Duncan told my mum about a leading light in the Canadian Communist Party, a Scot called Bill Findlay, who had gone out to Canada in the early 1920s. He had spent a year at the Lenin School in Moscow in 1931. He had been demobbed in Britain and had not gone back to Canada, somewhere along the line the party decided he should do that.

Kath Duncan approached my mother and asked if he could stay with us. Frankly, there was no room for him, but that is how the party was; it is my contention that they decided they didn't want my mum to be on her own but wanted a party bloke to go and live with her - and that is how it happened.

STALINIST MOULDING

He came to stay. There were my grandparents, my mum, brother and I in a small house in Brockley. He stayed with my mum until he died in 1982. It was a bad thing for many reasons. They never married, although there was a close relationship in the very early years; but it was one of those relationships that became a total disaster. There was no emotional commitment between the two of them, yet somehow she could never bring herself to end the relationship. The problem with him was that he was in his mid-40s when he came to stay and had never had a permanent relationship with anybody; he had become a party moron, and emotionally he was still a teenager until the end of life. He was a thorough political, personal and emotional Stalinist. There was not one ounce of humanity in the person and I had little time for him, and yet he was incredibly influential over me. To this day I know I still struggle against how I was shaped when I was young.

So we had this very odd situation where there was a lodger in the house who was this brooding Stalinist figure, who I came to realise was wrong on all the issues as far as I was concerned, right the way through to Czechoslovakia and the other great totem issues.

The party was born into a community, and if you think how many members the CP had in 1945 - about 60,000 - in areas like Deptford one in 25 people might be party members. But we were different, even though there were quite a lot of people around. As a small kid I went on demonstrations and my earliest political memory is in 1949, when I was five. There was a women's peace movement against militarism, and my mum, being a war widow, was quite involved in it. She was among a group of women who threw themselves in front of a tank going down Whitehall.

On another occasion we demonstrated in support of a CP woman called Pat Seers who had been in a cinema showing a film which portrayed Rommel favourably, and had disrupted the show - she was not only arrested for that but put in Holloway prison. My mum took me on a demonstration against this, with mostly women and kids, and we were coming up towards the prison when suddenly a load of police came out on horseback and literally charged into the crowd. I remember being dragged onto the kerb to avoid the police horses.

I also have a very clear memory, as a seven- or eight-year-old in the early 1950s, when the Cold War was beginning to build up, of a May Day march down Deptford High Street when I was marching behind the Deptford CP banner with my mum. There were blokes chanting, 'Ban communism now', and I turned around and made a two-fingered gesture to them, because it was clear what seemed right and wrong to me. It was obvious at school and in the neighbourhood that we were not in the political mainstream - the people living next door blanked us out because we were Communists.

My mum left the party in 1952, but remained a Communist. Although she is a hardliner, in many ways she is a humanitarian in the real sense. He was the sort of bloke who would have been a local police official in a communist state, but behind a desk. But Bill Findlay would have been the sort of official who organised neighbours to spy on each other. He would have seen nothing wrong with that because the party was all that mattered and the state had to be protected. The fact that he personified the party, together with cold war pressures, made it all wrong for my mother so she dropped out.

My grandmother looked after the home while my mother worked and was the breadwinner.

GROWING UP

In 1956 Bill had a heart attack. He smoked heavily, but I think Hungary and all that took a toll on him physically. One after another of his party members in his factory came to visit him and told him they were going to leave the party.

My mum remained committed to the broad idea of communism but she rejected the organisation. She drifted out of the party but never expressed public hostility and remained loyal where the Soviet Union was concerned. My brother never joined the YCL or had anything to do with it; he rejected it all when we were quite young.

I joined the YCL in 1959 when I was 15. The catalyst was that I got into a bit of trouble with the police. I had to do a year's probation. I was at home a bit more, reading the papers, and I think I suddenly grew up. The *Daily Worker* was always lying around and I had seen mention of the YCL so I joined. I hated school: I resented having to be there, hated institutional education. From the age of 14 I truanted a fair bit and I just got out at 15 as quickly as I could.

I started attending YCL meetings, and all my institutional being started to come out. It was the worst side of me, which I had absorbed from Bill, that communism was all about the party, discipline and order. The YCL was always organised like a junior Communist Party so I walked straight into this.

I had a formative experience in 1960. One of these Outward Bound courses came up at school and I thought it was a good skive - I could get a month off school - so I applied to go and was accepted. I went away to Lake Ullswater in the Lake District in February 1960 for a month. It was freezing and snowing. I came home with TB and pleurisy after which I was in hospital for four months.

I was only 16 and was in hospital all over that winter, and during that time all the First World War soldiers - who were now old men who had bad chests from going down the trenches - were coming in to die. I spent a lot of time talking to them and it was a very important period for me. I started reading and learning and making up for what I had missed at school.

My rebellion against what happened at home came later, because I had this split idea about communism: my father was a great hero but this lodger, who I could only think of as an uncompromising bastard, came out of the same tradition; so it was confusing. My mum was in the middle, and I was trying to make sense of it - and to this day I don't think I really have made sense of it. I went onto the national committee of the YCL in 1964; me and a friend went on together and they were fighting like mad to keep us off. A year earlier, my girlfriend Linda had become pregnant. She was 18 I was 19 and we got married, and I had two kids by the time I was 21 and a mortage and a house by 1965.

I was influenced by the 1960s because it meant an opening up and flowering of politics and the great thing for me was that I was young enough to want to change things that had been embedded in my mind in the 1950s. By 1966 I was ready to really junk it; The imprisonment of the writers Sinyafsky and Daniel in Russia was a catalyst for me, I was looking for a way out of the mindset.

'WHAT'S A BOUTIQUE?'

Because the YCL was made up of young people, we were naturally more influenced by what was going on around us. Nevertheless we were hostile to the hippy movement in many ways. We were hostile to drug taking and we didn't like flower power and meditation - but we saw the era as positive in terms of style and rebellion.

I wasn't really part of it at all. I had a mortgage and two kids so it passed me by in a way, although at the same time I was trying to address it. The party failed to address it at all. In 1966 there was a joint YCL-CP national executive committee and I went along to it. I was trembling but I made a contribution, after which John Gollan got up and said, 'Don't get above yourself'. All we had been talking about was that the YCL should somehow connect to youth culture.

In the middle of this, the industrial organiser, Bert Ramelson asked, 'What's a boutique?' He didn't even know what we were talking about, we were arguing that we should start boutiques and that sort of thing. They were so divorced from what was going on. They were sitting in King Street judging what was happening amongst young people in broad mass political terms, without any real feel or understanding about young people's lives or the things they were doing.

In south east London, where we had 350 YCL members, we were attempting to reach out to young people, but we couldn't throw ourselves into it because we were still a democratic centralist organisation. The YCL was bought and paid for by the Communist Party, the Communist Party was still bought and paid for by the Soviet Union we now find out - and where did you go with that?

In 1967 we produced this leaflet *The Trend - Communism*, it was a four-pager, we produced a million copies for a membership drive and we got a thousand new members. If you look at that leaflet today - it had a picture on it of a young woman in a stripey skirt which was below her knees, not how things actually were then, and a middle-aged bloke playing a trumpet, which wasn't the rock and roll of the time. Even there we didn't get it right, although we had The Who playing at the YCL Congress in Derbyshire in 1967. We started up Trend clubs, there was one in Wembley where a group called the Bow Street Runners used to play. They became very popular with 4-500 young people turning up every week. We started one in south east London which only lasted about three months.

What we were doing was trying to set up a piece of the action for ourselves. In December 1963 the Beatles played at Lewisham Odeon and *Challenge*, our paper, had a picture of the Beatles on the front page and an interview with them by Tom Spence. We got 500 copies of *Challenge*, went down to the Odeon and sold 250 copies, which we thought was fantastic. But the truth is that we were on the outside looking in - we weren't really integrated with young people.

The great thing about the YCL in the 1960s, which actually helped a lot of people like me to unload themselves of the worst of the baggage of communism of the 1940s and 1950s, was that it began to seriously question the class party line - we knew that young people did not go along with that and attempted to somehow at least address what was going on. When, early in 1967, the Action Programme of the Czech Communist Party was issued, we were all incredibly excited - here at last was a way that communism itself could be liberated from the worst elements of its own history, and at the same time it could become a new force for the future. Of course there was no way that could happen but we didn't realise that at the time. Even if Dubcek had seen it through, it still could not have worked, in my opinion, because it was still being done through a democratic centralist organisation. At the time I believed it was a great moment and even as late as 1977, when we had the British Road to Socialism revamp Congress, I was still full of hope.

That Congress finally disillusioned me. That debate went on for another two years before we were finally smashed into the ground when the leadership would not accept even the modest reforms in the minority report on inner party democracy in 1979. I decided at that time the party was dead and that nothing would change until something changed in the Soviet Union. I stayed a member, but resigned from the London district committee of the party, although I was still a party candidate as late as 1986 in Lewisham.

THE STATE OF REVOLUTION

Even when I think back to the years I spent in Lewisham when I was a party candidate - all my work in the community, all the housing cases I took up, the campaign on the local railway station was all geared up to me being the CP candidate, that's the truth of it. I am not saying what I did wasn't needed and that people weren't rehoused or the station kept open. The *Morning Star* gave me a weekly contact with a whole lot of people like tenants which kept you well in touch. But ultimately, it was all for the benefit of the party - in effect, we used people's problems.

We weren't a revolutionary party at all, and I was a member for 32 years, nearly half of its existence. We had the rhetoric, we talked about the class moving this and that, but we never saw it really in those terms. Even when we analysed our electoral work, which I now look back on as a complete waste of time, we presented the lowest common denominator of the argument: that we were part of the anti-Tory movement and a lot of people who couldn't bring themselves to vote Communist would be stimulated to vote Labour, so we were vital to help return Labour candidates. To some extent that is true, my great moment was getting nearly 500 votes in the east Lewisham constituency and people saying to me there was absolutely no doubt I had helped Labour get elected. But what is revolutionary about that? There is nothing revolutionary about helping to change the complexion of Parliament.

Many party members were helping people take charge of their own lives, in the sense that they should struggle and not just sit back and accept things. This was despite the 'Moscow Gold' revelations and the lies we got from people who ran the party all those years and conned us and ripped us off - I have got nothing but the deepest and utter contempt for those people. But I am no more going to let them rob me of the way I felt politically than I would let the class enemy do it, if you like.

What the party gave me was not what a group of corrupt full-time officials presented. It gave me an idea about struggle, about empowerment, it gave me a sense of class loyalty - which has become less and less relevant in the sense that the world has changed and you've had to re-adapt. In those terms the party was providing something useful.

However, I still think the party was an aberration because I don't think we ever needed the Communist Party. The CP was a Bolshevik imposition on the British socialist movement; we were part of Lenin's split. And yet I gave the best years of my life to something which was objectively destructive to socialism. It undermined, for 70-odd years, a re-assessment of social democracy.

A DECENT BURIAL

I retrained as a journalist and in 1988 went on a three year stint as a freelance in Bulgaria. On my return I turned down the chance to work on one of the *Financial Times'* business magazines. The point was, having ended all those years in the print, having established myself in journalism, I was about to start a second career but I decided not to do that.

Instead I went to work at *New Times* the paper of the Democratic Left. I thought that if we didn't win that battle in the party and put it to bed and give it as decent a burial as it deserved and we keep all those resources and money out of the hands of the tankies and Stalinists, they would carry on wreaking damage throughout the labour movement.

I feel pleased that I have done something useful and my politics in the end did come up to something. The Democratic Left, with all its weaknesses and problems, is doing a much more useful job with what was left of the resources of the old CP. Being involved in the Democratic Left was the most enormous political therapy, which saved me from having a political nervous breakdown. You can't be free of your background, it is what you are and your whole make-up; the question is whether or not you can somehow live with it psychologically as well as politically, and live with it in a way that allows you to re-humanise yourself. That is the struggle I am going through, to try and find out what parts of me I buried for the party.

I split up with Linda in 1980. We still keep in touch. Since then our kids have grown up; my daughter has two kids of her own and my son is making his way in the world. Fortunately, because we were young and hard-up, we shared a house with my mum when my kids were growing up, so that created quite a bond, which remains to this day. Every week my mum visits Julie and the kids, they go out and do things, and sometimes there are four generations involved altogether. It is a positive set of relationships. We are all gradually having to overcome the effects of being a 'communist family' - still a very difficult task.

MARTIN KETTLE is an assistant editor of the Guardian *newspaper. He was brought up in Leeds where his parents were active CP members. His father, Arnold Kettle, was a member of the CP national executive for over 12 years.*

A SPECIAL INHERITANCE

I have no doubt at all that it is a special inheritance; we are marked for life and there is no point in denying it. It seems to live with me a lot of the time even though my direct experience of the party is quite limited. I was a member of the party when I was a student, but I haven't been a member since 1971, and I never thought of myself as a particularly dedicated, still less disciplined, party member. It was very much a parental experience.

I think they very much wanted a cause to believe in, a cause to which they could dedicate themselves, to be members of something which gave them a compass and a certainty about a world which was collapsing. My parents joined the CP in the 1930s. My father joined in about 1936 at Cambridge, the classic Cambridge communist experience; my mother joined as a student at Edinburgh. They met during the war in the NUS as student militants.

My judgement is that they wanted a church, they wanted a religion. I think they would vehemently deny this but I think, in retrospect, that is what they wanted. It gave to them the sense of being part of something glorious, fulfilling, ideal and wonderful, and international, within which their own lives and attitudes made sense. Specifically, it was the anti-fascist movement where they both came in, and that huge contempt for the British ruling class and the way it handled fascism. Munich in particular, an event about which my parents could not speak with anything other than total contempt, that was very formative for them.

Eric Hobsbawm, in his book on the twentieth century, now calls the Cold War a religious war, and that is a brave self-perception in this late stage of his life. There is faith or loyalty involved, although it differs from case to case; and the big misconception in my own experience. or that of my parents, as transmitted to me, is that the loyalty was to the Soviet Union.

I think my parents were much more loyal to the British Communist Party than they were to the Soviet Union, and they were sceptics about the Soviet Union from the 1950s onwards. They were certainly not 100 per cent right down the line on Hungary and by the time you get to the trials of the writers Daniel and Sinyavsky in Russia in 1964, and then the treatment of Solzhenitsyn, and then Czechoslovakia, they were deeply critical. They still tended to defend the Soviet Union, in the sense of saying, 'You have got to understand how they see it', but it wasn't a case of, 'If the Soviet Union says it it must be right and we must say that'.

But they did have a loyalty to the party - which, although the party saw itself in an international context, was a very British organisation; my sense of communism is very much British communism and the British CP, with the particular cultural characteristics that organisation had.

I felt that the Soviet Union was misunderstood as a child and I was conscious of that at school. I was not brought up with a reverential attitude to the Soviet Union, though the first public event I can remember was the death of Stalin. When you consider that happened in the year of the coronation, on the whole English people of my generation might remember the coronation. I don't, I remember the death of Stalin. My early years are punctuated by those sorts of events. I can remember Khrushchev's secret speech. I can remember Hungary but I can't remember Suez.

A MISSIONARY ZEAL

I think my parents saw themselves, certainly in my mother's case, as bringing good news to the masses. She had a missionary zeal. But not in the sense of bombarding people with leaflets; on the contrary, she would explain to people how sensible communists were and what nice people they were, people like you and me. Any support my mother got from standing in elections was entirely due to the fact that people liked and admired her as a person, and not in any sense because they wanted to support the British Communist Party.

The Communist Party was very socially conservative and that

became painfully true in the 1960s, which the CP had terrible difficulties adjusting to.

My father, Arnold Kettle, was on the executive committee of the CP from before Hungary until after Czechoslovakia, about 12 to 14 years, and he was a pretty serious figure. He was away periodically, although I don't think of him being away a huge amount; it was always an event when he went to London. He went with Bert Ramelson, who also went from Leeds, where I was brought up. Bert and he would go down on the train together and come back on the train together. We would often go to meet them at Leeds Central Station and I have a memory of steam trains arriving there and my father and Bert coming through the steam. Edward Thompson told me years later that quite often there would be impromptu gatherings at the station of communists who wanted to know what had happened at the executive committee and, in 1956, rows and arguments took place on the station platform itself.

My mother, Margot Kettle, was on the Yorkshire district committee and was very much involved in the party at a local level in Leeds. She stood as a candidate in various parts of Leeds. My parents were in different CP branches, my father was in the university branch and my mother in a geographical branch, so I guess they didn't go to meetings together. They probably organised it so we always had a parent at home.

I was very conscious of the party and it was a social network. My parents were friends of a lot of the leading people in the party, in particular the Gollans. My mother and Elsie Gollan were best friends. We used to stay with the Gollans when we came to London and, on the rare occasions when they came to Leeds, they stayed with us. My recollections of these people were as parental friends - there is a picture of me doing a jigsaw with Harry Pollitt. I have very much a sense of the party as an extended family, which was rocked by 1956 when we suddenly stopped seeing the people I thought were our friends, and I didn't understand why.

We used to regularly go to Halifax to see the Thompsons, Edward and Dorothy Thompson, and they left in 1956. We stopped seeing them. I didn't realise that had happened. I just remember saying, 'Why don't we ever see the Thompsons any more?' Their son Mark Thompson was the same age as me and we used to play together. I subsequently realised that my father actually voted on the EC against support for the invasion of Hungary; he was in a minority of two with Gollan, which is interesting. My father stayed in but a lot of his friends left - and some of our personal friends rather than prominent Communists.

We often went on holidays with communists. We went to Scotland or Cornwall with the Gollans regularly, but we didn't go to Eastern Europe. My parents, and particularly my father, had this love affair with Italy, and he wanted to go to Italy as often as he possibly could; and Yugoslavia, where he had been in the war; our holidays increasingly took us to Yugoslavia. From 1960 onwards we went there three or four times and we went with another family from Leeds who were communists.

I can remember a Christmas when my father wasn't there because he was in Cuba. I remember being sad that he wasn't around but, equally, I was very interested that he was on a delegation that met Castro and Che Guevara. I have a picture of my father with Che Guevara. The Cubans were the glamorous side of the movement and it is easily forgotten now that the Cubans gave this cause a lot of street credibility in the 1960s, which it might not have had but for the Cuban revolution. Castro was glamorous and a role model in a way that Khrushchev barely was and Brezhnev certainly wasn't. The great hero to me was Yuri Gagarin because he was glamorous and he'd done this amazing thing, he smiled and he was young. I had pictures of Gagarin on my wall. I didn't have pictures of Khrushchev on my wall, it would never have occured to me, and still less pictures of Lenin or Stalin. I took Gagarin down when I put up the first Rolling Stones picture.

I had the illusion when I was young that the party was much more important and widespread than it was. I can remember at school saying to a teacher when I was seven, 'You don't know who John Gollan is?' Of course the teacher didn't know, and I was really surprised about that because I thought of him in the same league of importance as Gaitskell: he was a party leader - I didn't realise he was in a very small party.

I think my parents were both very loyal to the party as an institution, they gave a lot of time, money and emotion to the party. It was an intellectual household and there was a lot of discussion; ideas were being batted around a lot in my childhood, although the party position tended to be taken fairly much for granted as being right - but not swallowed whole. The Labour Party was the enemy and there was a sense of superiority towards the Labour Party.

A lot of people came through our house, which was a big house. They stayed at our house and came for meetings, and I have a vivid sense of the party as being of all social backgrounds and of all the nationalities who passed through our house. We had Russians and Third World students who visited, we knew Africans and Asians at a time when not many other people did. We had an Indian lodger who was a Communist, and I was quite aware of the Third World at the age of 10 or 11.

Because my father was relatively well known, and our name was unusual, quite a few people knew who Kettle; and I still meet people who tell me things I didn't know about his reputation in Leeds. I can remember trying to get people at school to come on a demonstration and they were a bit hesitant about it - this was against the imprisonment of Nelson Mandela in 1965. I managed to get one person to join me, and I can remember several people saying no. I still keep in touch with the one, he's a rich solicitor living in Surrey, but still Labour. My father's impact on me was very great. He was a good writer, not a good speaker, but very highly regarded, and I got a lot of kudos out of that, I took pride in that.

DRIFTING AWAY

I was never in the YCL, although I always considered myself on the left. I did discuss joining the YCL with my mother and she said it was up to me, and I shouldn't join anything until I became a student. Then I went away to become a student and I did join the CP, and in retrospect I think that the party was something to cling onto. It was such a trauma leaving home that joining the CP wasn't so much about becoming an adult as staying a child.

We had a small branch of students in Oxford where I was, and most of the people there who came from communist families came from much harder line families. I immediately felt out of place because I always felt much more of a libertarian socialist; my emotional sympathies were totally with the 1968 movement internationally. I was born in 1949. I was taken to Aldermaston when I was little and we did something called the March for Life. I did the march three or four times, including on my own with a friend when I was 13. We went to demonstrations at the Labour Party conference in Blackpool - it was a day out - and the late 1960s and the student movement became an extension of that. Culturally, CND was important for me and then came the Vietnam Solidarity Campaign(VSC). I supported the VSC line of 'Victory to the NLF', whereas the basic CP line was 'Peace in Vietnam'. We were on Ho Chi Minh's side and I was very excited by student sit-ins and the 1968 stuff. I set off in a battered van with some friends to go to Paris after hearing about the student riots, but we didn't get there because we forgot our passports!

On Czechoslovakia I was totally in the Dubcek camp, and I found the Prague Spring an incredibly exciting development because he offered the prospect of the kind of human development of socialism I would have liked to have seen. It didn't happen but I identified with that and I began to drift away from the party; as I grew up I didn't need it. My parents had a lot of Czech friends. A close friend of my mother's was Dubcek's foreign minister, Jiri Hayek, who had been a political refugee here during the second world war. The only thing I have joined since has been the Labour Party, of which I have been an inactive member. I felt with the CP that it was dying away.

I can remember my father saying, years ago, that the trouble with the communist parties of western Europe was that they all got stuck at the start of the Cold War and that was where they now were, and that was true. They continued to draw on the support they already had for 20 years, between 1948-68, there was an amazing consistency electorally and nothing changed. After 1968 they began to decline because they couldn't command the loyalty of the post-war generation.

Our parent's generation had incredible historical luck to be young at a time when the issues of the world were very polarised. It was very dangerous but you could take a side, one or the other, and the prospect of your side winning was serious. And if your side won then something really glorious could happen to the whole world. They lived with that possibility. If you look historically, that opportunity occurs incredibly infrequently, it is like being French in 1789. Most people don't have that, they don't have death or glory problems. As well as that, their generation had the war and they won, and that was an immense thing for them. I feel burdened by that history - they set a standard that was not repeatable and we just have to do the best we can with a different situation.

My father knew some of the Cambridge spies of the 1930s. The first book that came out about Anthony Blunt didn't name Blunt but it said there was a fourth man. I remember mentioning this to my father and he said, 'It will be Anthony Blunt.' A few weeks later it *was* Anthony Blunt, so I think he knew quite a lot. I don't know what he knew exactly, but certainly he knew Guy Burgess and I think a good friend of my father's recruited Burgess to the party, Brian Simon. My father understood the position of the spies. I can remember him saying, 'We thought Chamberlain was the traitor'. I don't know what role James Klugmann had in all that, but clearly he had a role, and Klugmann and my father were quite close friends.

My father was once asked by the Soviet embassy to find out something about engineering products that were being produced in some factory in Leeds. He told my brother he debated about what he should do, and in the end he wrote to the company and did it completely openly - he said 'I have been asked by the Soviet embassy to ask you ...' I don't think that was his scene at all.

I can remember being very mystified as to why my parents were so hostile to Churchill. When he died in 1965, the *Morning Star* ran a very hostile coverage and I thought: you guys have been telling me all the time that this man made great speeches during the war and you listened to them; he spoke for Britain and he was a great man. I thought there was a meanness of spirit, and I just felt more sympathetic to the modern world.

Another person I disagreed with my parents about was Kennedy. I thought Kennedy was a great man and he represented a lot of things that I believed in, and I admired him. Kennedy's assassination was a terrible event and I still cannot watch that film of him being killed. I find it shattering because it sums up for me the death of an innocence. I agree he was much more right-wing than I realised, and I shouldn't have idealised him in this way, but like a lot of people I had a great feeling for Kennedy.

I do think the music coming out of America in the early 1960s - some of which was approved by the party, like Pete Seeger, early Bob Dylan - had a tremendous resonance for me. Someone put on an early Joan Baez album where I was the other day and I was very moved by it. It was the music associated with the civil rights movement and Martin Luther King; that mattered a lot to me and I have a big emotional response to all that. Unlike the communists who felt Dylan betrayed the purity of what he was doing by going electric in 1964, I liked it.

KILLING WITH KINDNESS

I now firmly believe that the Communist Party killed my development with kindness. I think it was a very benevolent, all-involving experience but, ultimately, it denied the individual. I think it made you feel you were a part of something bigger, and it stopped you feeling you were a person who had a right to work things out yourself, to be yourself and to sort out your own feelings: because in some senses it always encouraged you to lose yourself in the bigger picture.

It was not tyrannical in an overt sense, but it definitely had that stifling effect on me, and I know other people who feel it had that effect too. I feel that very, very deeply - I have talked to pyschoanalysts about it - and it is a very repressive thing in all kinds of well-intentioned ways. My parents would be deeply shocked to hear me say these things. It was a form of shielding from the realities of life, and it also made you underrate the importance of what you thought yourself and of yourself. There was always something bigger going on which was more important. You felt it was wrong to be too concerned about yourself - there was the party, the movement, history. Marxism had painted this picture in which you didn't have to examine things yourself, and to do so was a bit of a diversion. That was an immensely repressive thing for me as a human being, although

I have a great sense of affection for the party in lots of ways.

Our parents always said, when something was wrong, 'But you have to think about the Soviet Union and the international situation' - so you could never actually say it was wrong. You were always backing off saying what you thought. You found it difficult to express yourself and find yourself; and we all have to do that so it has taken us a lot longer, in fact it is still going on for me. In some ways these are things I have only become aware of in the last year or two. It has left huge marks on me. I have never felt that I was on the right, even if other people think I have moved to the right - and in a way I have. I still think of myself as being on the left and cannot imagine being anything else.

I feel a responsibility that my children have an interest in public affairs. I want them to know about politics and public policy issues and I want them to recognise the high importance of those things. But I am pretty sure my children wouldn't be able to tell you what left-wing means, whereas I could have certainly told you that at their age.

CONCLUSION

Ultimately, the pretence proved too much for the idealism, and an organisation which did not question itself sufficiently ceased to be. During its existence, the Communist Party had an enormous impact on the lives of its members and their families. The childhoods described in this book were often full of paradoxes as we tried to make sense of and live with competing strands of bohemianism and puritanism, of sociability and togetherness within the party yet separateness and difference from the wider society. It is perhaps not surprising that more than one person described it as 'like a religion'. A picture emerges of parents driven by compassion and idealism who strove to build a better world for all but who could be absent and distant from their own children in the cause of the greater good.

For those brought up within the CP family, we tend to underestimate the current sense of loss, not so much at losing a party and a programme, but an essence of ourselves, in my case some of my own childhood. In this book people have spoken about the sacrifices demanded by the CP and readily accepted by its members, if not their families. But the party did not just take from people, it gave them a great deal as well. It gave them a community, but also a value-base and attitudes, some of which have proved to be enduring. These are about being part of, and feeling some responsibility for, what goes on in the world. It is a continuation of the theme of striving for something better, albeit perhaps now on a more individualistic basis.

Many, as they moved out of childhood, chose occupations characterised by intellectual creativity and expression. The decline in traditional industries and greater educational opportunities may have something to do with this trend (and there are of course others in non-professional jobs that I have not spoken to) but many people in this book speak of the importance given to discussion and intellectual debate in CP families. Among the people interviewed here are academics, writers, journalists and poets; there are teachers, lobbyists and entertainers also.

The CP experience has probably also left its mark on our attitude to politics in general. We are wary of 'having all the answers', and like many of our generation are less likely to seek the betterment of society through organised political parties. Our approach to political activity is jaundiced by our CP background. Ideas about feminism, race equality, democratic participation and avoiding 'cult of the leader' have all meant that there is much greater scepticism of political rhetoric and propaganda.

The experience of Thatcherism and the supremacy of the New Right in the 1980s led to a disillusionment with the political process that has affected many who consider themselves on the political left. Idealism has been out of fashion, but it may yet re-appear in the future. The CP may be no more but some of its values live on.